The Sea Changes

To Marilyn & Pat

Enjoy

Nancy Charley

xx

Also by Nancy Charley from Eagle's Nest Publishing

Non-Fiction
Being Church

Poetry
Apprentice
Patricia's Box
Journeywoman
Dead to Fire

The Sea Changes

Musings from a beach hut

on Tankerton Slopes

Nancy Charley

Eagle's Nest Publishing

Eagle's Nest Publishing, 11 Hillyfield Road, Ashford, Kent,
TN23 4QL
First published in Great Britain by Eagle's Nest, 2017

ISBN: 978-1-326-92989-3

The Sea Changes

Nancy Charley was writer-in-residence at the *Little Blue Hut* from 12th September to 26th October, 2011, courtesy of Canterbury City Council. Her aim for the residency was to consider colours and how they change, and to develop these musings into poetry. But with time to 'stand and stare' Nancy discovered many things about coastal life. *The Sea Changes* recounts these discoveries and the joy and motivation they've given. Nancy grew up in the Midlands, and graduated from the University of Newcastle-upon-Tyne in Medical Sciences. She lived in Ramsgate for more than twenty years but in 2014, moved to Ashford, Kent. She currently works as the Archivist for the Royal Asiatic Society

In memory of my mum,
Mary Beasley,
who taught me so much,
equipped me to learn more.

Acknowledgements

With grateful thanks to *Creative Canterbury* of Canterbury City Council for the award of the residency at the Little Blue Hut, Tankerton Slopes, near Whitstable.

Thanks also to Jeremy Langrish and to Jane Findlay, Jo Field, Margaret Swan, Marilyn Donovan and Sindonia Tyrell of the Bellyful for their continued support in all my writing endeavours.

And to my family – who make/made me what I am.

Contents

At Sea

I'm at a loss to describe the sea; metaphors I dream up seem demeaning, for even when it's calm, lapping, quilted (there, I'm already belittling – the sea as bed covering) it amazes me.

As for stormy days when the lion roars, white horses dance or a bull rampages – these clichés are but poor imitation. And if I try to name its hue – it is green, jade, grey, brown, blue, iridescent and drab – a seascape shifts with such rapidity that a single shade fails to convey any reality.

It's a bit like making God in our image – controlling who she'll be, or pigeon-holing our friend/neighbour/work-colleague/the immigrant who dared to come, into that type of person.

Sea – it leaves me speechless, awed, in love. I guess there is the nub – like love, the sea cannot be fathomed, understood.

Town Girl by the Sea

As I drive towards the beach hut a rhyme threads through my mind: "What is this life if, full of care, / We have no time to stand and stare?" It is a poignant reminder of my mother – lines she often quoted, but rarely seemed to live by. In fact, she probably knew all the words of *Leisure*.[1] In the weeks before she died, aged 79, she was still singing French songs she'd learnt at school; weeks spent, energy-permitting, sorting and reallocating a lifetime's possessions.

Such need of busyness became inculcated in me. I've raised five children and cared for a variety of people whose paths have intertwined with mine. There has always been something that needed planning, sorting, making or doing. But over recent years I've had to learn that if I am serious about creative writing I need to 'idle': lie in the bath, walk, sit, daydream and encourage my brain to switch off from efficient organisation mode. Then ideas may germinate; phrases, characters and plots find room to breathe which may eventually blossom into poems, stories and plays. At last – a fantastic opportunity to 'stand and stare' – six weeks as writer-in-residence of a beach hut.

The Little Blue Hut is at Tankerton, which lies between Whitstable and Herne Bay on the North Kent coast. From 2009-2012 the hut was provided as a residency by *Creative Canterbury*, part of Canterbury City Council, and writers, photographers, painters, printers, a lyricist and a theatre company have all enjoyed the privilege of letting its sea views influence their inspiration. It is perched back row, end of line, number 139, on a steepish grassy incline between Marine Terrace and the promenade. This slope is zig-zagged by various paths and steps, and splodged with brightly coloured beach huts.

My residency application stated:

> Though a writer, I've become fascinated by colour... The challenge is to present the wonder of colour in words, without using tired clichés or stating bald facts...
>
> I want to learn how to make a visual image into a tantalising word image, allowing colours and scenes to germinate in me so they take on their own significance. I want to wrestle with how to form, shape and use words to evoke what I am seeing...
>
> A residency in a beach hut on Tankerton Slopes would be ideal for this creative exploration. I would be able to commit a chunk of time to laying some

foundations in my thinking and practice. That would be really satisfying.

I didn't like art at school. It was a subject I dropped as soon as I was allowed. Consequently, my vocabulary and understanding of colour stayed stunted at around primary school level. So, I can name the colour of my beach hut as pastel or baby blue, and the neighbouring one royal blue with a white band, but nature – well, it's never a single block of colour. Even the grass isn't just green. And as for the sea, sky, sunsets… How can I possibly describe the colour-mixes and the wonders of how these can change in moments?

My knowledge of the sea and coast is also fairly rudimentary. I grew up in the Midlands. Each summer we stayed with my grandparents at St Annes-on-Sea, Lancashire, for a fortnight. Later in our childhoods we went to a Pontins or Butlins holiday camp. But though we were at the seaside, we didn't spend hours on the beach – perhaps a couple each afternoon. We'd build sandcastles, paddle but never swim, play hide-and-seek in the dunes, and I'd fly stunt kites with my brother. But I don't remember exploring, beachcombing or identifying finds.

I arrived in Ramsgate with three children, all under-fives, and two more were born there. My five children have spent most or all their childhoods by the sea. But I'm a town girl, a Midlander. As a conscientious mum wanting to entertain and occupy her children, I enjoyed the beach's usefulness as a place for picnics, sandcastles, building channels, beach cricket, French cricket, volleyball… But I'd never invested much time into learning about the environment.

I know a little: the tide's ebbs and flows are affected by the moon; cloud type can be an indicator of weather to come; gulls are coastal birds that nest on rooftops and pinch food from people sitting at seaside cafés… An elementary appreciation.

However, I've already begun to be more curious. Wandering along the Ramsgate coast has become a way to clear my head, think through 'what comes next' or simply to de-stress. And as I've started to draft a radio play in which a woman walks by the sea and offloads her worries to the waves, so I've needed to pay more attention to its many sights and sounds.

My intention for my time at the Little Blue Hut is to contemplate colour but I discover so much more.

Beach Huts

It's my first day. I park on Marine Parade and walk down the steps towards the hut. Mitch, from Creative Canterbury, has organised the residency for me, so I'm not sure whether I'm to meet a man or woman. No-one's here. I gaze on the sea – it laps at the shingle but I can't tell whether it's ebbing or flowing. I make a mental note to find out about tide times.

A few minutes later, a lady lollops down the slope. It seems one of those strange laws of design – no matter at what distance steps are placed they're never quite the right length to match your stride. Mitch has keys in hand and an enthusiastic greeting on her lips. Unlocking the door, she proceeds with a lesson in shutters – first take down the glass ones inside so you can unbolt the wooden ones that swing outwards; then replace the glass ones so the space is light-filled but stays warm and dry. The hut is furnished with a table, a couple of upright chairs, a comfy chair, a rug, mirror and some shelves with an accumulation of previous occupants' leavings. Three walls are white but one has been painted deep blue and decorated with chalk people. As Mitch chats about making the hut my own, I make another mental note to bring cloth and cleaning spray.

Mitch departs and I rearrange the furniture, putting the table by the windows so I'll be able to watch and write. I clear some of the things off the shelf into an empty Cadbury's Roses tin, stack others in a box, and then go back to my car to unload the boot. I bring blanket and towel, thick cardigan and raincoat, flip-flops, deckchair, bottles of water and cola, and bags of books – a dictionary, thesaurus, poetry books to inspire, nature and science books to inform.

Beach huts evolved from Victorian horse-drawn bathing carriages in which ladies and gentlemen journeyed from shore to wave, separately of course, getting changed into their bathing costumes on the way. The cold sea cure was a remedy for all kinds of ailments. As the English became less prudish the need for carriages diminished but it was still useful to have somewhere near the beach for changing and to brew a good cup of tea. Love for the huts has waxed and waned over the years.

Their heyday was in the post-war 1950s when the beaches had been cleared of barbed wire defences and people flocked to the coast for a seaside holiday.[1] Currently their popularity is peaking again and the ones at Tankerton sell for £15-25,000 or more. Besides this purchase price, there is ground rent to pay annually to the council or to private owners. Canterbury City Council has 630 beach huts sited on the North Kent coast, 382 of which are at Tankerton.[2]

An expensive garden shed on props – for that is all they really are. In fact if you pause to think about them, they are quite improbable things. In one of my writing groups we decide to respond to Frank W. Harvey's poem, *Ducks*, [3] which begins: "From troubles of the world I turn to ducks,/ Beautiful comical things…" Living in my beach hut world I create:

Beach Huts

Fed up with serious stuff I turn to beach huts,
their sheer audacity when propped on slopes
as though a judging panel prepared to vote
on the sea's performance.

They're brightly painted with stripes and shells,
mermaids, crossbones or candyfloss clouds
and with shutters, locks and bars
so nothing escapes when no-one's about.

Square containers for paraphernalia:
deckchairs, buckets, spades and lilos,
picnic baskets, surfboards, wind-up radios,
towels, kites, inflatable dodos

for the boxed seaside experience.
Hides from which to stand and stare
at untamed sea and windswept sky:
Englishmen's castles – Canute style.

Beach huts seem to invite a quirky creativity. Mine is uniformly pastel blue and unimaginatively named, Little Blue Hut, but others are covered in bold stripes and patterns, decorated with shells and mermaids, have shutters turned into sunglasses, and one is decked out as a pirate's den. Then there are the names – some inspired by the sea: Becalmed, The World is your Oyster, Seaways; some by the owner's name: Jenny Wren's Nest, Charlie's Plaice, Soozut; the jokey: Jabba, Madanha, Life Begins at 40 (on hut number 40) and the completely obscure: Kassita Jula, Oumadjani. Not all are painted – there are a few au naturelle allowing wood to weather in the salt-laden breeze. And not all are well-cared for; some have peeling paint and flapping roof-felt and look as if they haven't been inhabited for years.

According to my contract I'm not allowed in the hut after 11pm nor can I use cooking equipment. I wonder if these are general rules. Maybe if my residency had been in high summer I'd have heard people sleeping in huts or at least partying late into the night. One of my disappointments is how little they seem to be used – so many stay shuttered, barred and locked.

As for no cooking; I decide that rule is specific to my terms and conditions when I discover a burnt-down hut – all that remains on the black, charred ground are a kettle, a couple of pans and some cushions with obviously effective fire-resistant covers and foam. The huts on either side stand like stage sets; each has a missing wall revealing their inner worlds.

Though many owners seem reluctant to visit their huts, other people appropriate them. Toddlers love running up and down steps and playing peek-a-boo through railings, a hidden picnicking family is betrayed by the dad's Day-Glo pink T-shirt, and photographers line up huts in camera viewfinders.

For those who want sea views, but are disinclined to rough it in a humble hut, they can rent Beacon House.[4] Set on the hill behind the promenade, this wood-clad cottage painted cream is a bit of a holiday dream. One day I find a film crew in situ. Later that evening I walk with a friend on the shingle spit that appears at low tide. As we turn to head back for the shore, Beacon House is lit by stage-lights that stream out from the door and front windows, and are so bright that the trees behind appear as eerie luminous tresses. The house has become a premature Halloween mask. I wonder if the crew are aware of the drama they've created outside whilst busily filming indoors.

Beach hut life suits me. I begin to settle in.

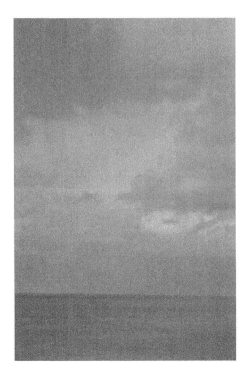

Settling In

The animals went in two by two, hurrah, hurrah…[1]

Another day and another phrase plucked from my childhood runs through my head. It's not prompted by an endless stream of animals, but by the parade of people on the promenade which separates the slope from the beach. Infrequently a solitary individual or a group appear but the majority walk in pairs. Some have made it into my notes:

Two yummy mummies jog by with buggies.

> Two striding Asian men; one with a hat that wants to fly. Walking back, they are laden with Tesco carrier bags.
>
> Two large men loafing.
>
> A mother and teenage daughter; the daughter trailing behind. On their return the mother, at the end of her tether, strains on an invisible leash.
>
> A couple, each with a buggy. When they sit on the grass near the hut and take the babies out for a cuddle, I discover they are new-born twins.

I've been watching the sea and sky, trying to think about colour changes, but my eye gets drawn to people. From my viewpoint, those walking east are usually announced by their shadows before they appear past the beach huts. I'm a nosy parker; unceasingly curious about people. I like to imagine the characters and stories behind faces and body postures. Sitting in the beach hut is like being in a hide from which I can observe the 'wildlife'.

I am satisfied with my own company, but this abundance of couples provokes the desire to share discoveries with a friend. As if on cue a spider crawls out from behind the window frame reminding me of Anansi (or in Southern USA, Aunt Nancy), the story-filled, trickster spider. I smile at the suitability of my companion.

Two older couples from a front-row beach hut enjoy the September sunshine; the men drink lager from cans and relax in deckchairs. One lady is busy taking photographs; the other's happy to sit and chat. Then one of the men unfurls a kite – a fluttery thing with no struts and a single string. As it is lifted by the wind, it's revealed as a chain of six flat jellyfish. The sixth tiniest fish twirls and pirouettes, and the kite creates delightful shadow patterns on the shingle. A woman takes the string and the jellyfish continue to wobble in their flight.

I look down to make notes and on looking up again I find a jellyfish escape under way. They are dashing across the shingle headed for the sea. The man rushes to retrieve them as they are restrained by the groyne. He ambles back, winding string, but just as he is about to reach his companions, the jellyfish dash off again. This time he runs to recover them and makes sure he holds on tight till they are safely inside their beach hut.

I notice the kite and people's clothes, like the beach huts, are solid blocks of colour and therefore much easier to describe even if they are multi-coloured. The sea is so variable with shades of this and hints of that, and changes as the sun comes out or as clouds create shadows. I've bought some books about colour to read during my residency. I discover that I am not the only one who has trouble; through history, colours have changed names, importance and symbolism and it seems there have always been difficulties in defining all the different variations:

> Languages have never been used for labelling more than a fraction of the millions of colour-sensations which most of us are perfectly well-equipped to enjoy and, we might suppose name… modern colour systems, following the lead of James Clark Maxwell in the 1860s, have usually resorted to numbers in order to distinguish perceptible difference of hue or value

> (lightness or darkness) in what has turned out to be a far from symmetrical colour space.[2]

The same book, *Colour and Meaning* by John Gage, also informs me that colour traditionally has been considered a feminine attribute in Western art. But before I can take feminist umbrage I read there may be some scientific reasoning behind this: Caucasian males are 100 times more likely to suffer from some form of colour-blindness than are females.[3] That gives me cause for thought and one of those unanswerable questions surfaces: How can we know if how I see green is the same as how you see green?

I read on. Gage tells me that the most widely recognised colour-continuum is the spectrum of light we see in a rainbow. This was identified by Isaac Newton in the seventeenth century. Yet the number and order to these colours have been disputed; even Newton kept changing his mind and eventually opted for the seven colour version so that it would be in harmony with a musical octave.[4] We remember the colours with the mnemonics ROY G BIV or Richard Of York Gave Battle In Vain. The book suggests that the bands blend into each other making it difficult to discern where one ends and the next begins or even if all the colours are present. A secondary rainbow always has its colours reversed.

The first Sunday of my residency I can't go to the beach hut because I need to take two of my sons back to their universities. As I head for home there is a rain squall. Suddenly I am driving towards a double rainbow. It's true. It is difficult to define the bands and at times the indigo and violet don't appear. And the secondary rainbow has its colours reversed. I'd never noticed before. Like so many things, once you know it's obvious…

In these first days, I'm unsure whether I will be able to come to any conclusions regarding colour or if any poetry will emerge from this 'set-aside' time. I write in my journal: I am unsure of why I am here – other than the sheer joy of being here. I have fallen in love with the routine of taking time to sit, watch and think in this conducive environment. On my very first day I stay to see the sunset and I'm treated to a spectacular display of colour change. As the sun sinks in the west in a panoply of gold, yellow, tangerine, rose and mauve, a full moon rises in the east until they hang opposed. This is how it always is, I naively suppose.

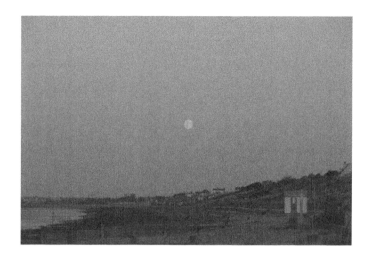

Moon Shine Moon Time

The man in the moon came down too soon, and asked his way to Norwich,
He went by the south and burnt his mouth by eating cold plum porridge.
Traditional[1]

It is a most beautiful and delightful sight to behold the body of the Moon.
Galileo Galilei[2]

I swivel from west to east and back again, camera in hand. In the west, the sun – a golden coin tinged with white – is surrounded by a rich yellow, tangerine and rose pink sky. As it dips towards the horizon, a mauve haze and low-lying clouds create a moody contrast to the sun's dazzle. This is a sunset worth gazing on. In the east, a full white moon rises against a backdrop which could be called 'sky-blue-pink'. The sun sets and the colours begin to fade. It's not instantaneous. Sunset doesn't mean immediate darkness but the gradual gathering gloom of twilight turning into night. I watch the moon's ascent in the sky. It's so bright I can see some of its features even without binoculars or telescope. As the sky darkens, the moon takes on a yellow hue with splashes of white.

Simultaneous sunset and moonrise – this is how day and night are separated. Or not! I have to admit, before this residency, I only knew about the moon's monthly wax and wane. Some days later I arrive at the beach hut on a bright, sunny morning; a white-lace moon hangs in the sky. I've seen the moon during the day on a few other occasions and thought that it was some peculiarity. Whilst on the Internet finding out the local tide times, I also search for sun and moon rise and set times. Google provides.[3] The sun I discover, as it heads for the autumn equinox and beyond, will rise about three minutes later and set about three minutes earlier each day. But the moon has a very different story.

The moon is Earth's only natural satellite and it is in orbit about 238,856 miles (384,401km) from the earth. It rotates around the earth in approximately 29.5 days – about a month – the word month originating from that of the moon. It also rotates on its own axis in a similar amount of time so that, on the earth, we always see the same face of the moon. Because these rotations are so aligned there really is, to us, a dark side of the moon.[4]

The moon is not a source of light. It reflects the sun. Moon rise happens about 50 minutes later each day because of its orbit round the earth, and it appears to us in its various phases – new moon, waxing crescent, quarter moon, waxing gibbous, full moon, waning gibbous, quarter and crescent – due to the relative positions of the sun, earth and moon. Revolutions upon revolutions.

At new moon the sun and moon, from the earth, are in the same direction in the sky and so the moon is hidden. As the moon's orbit progresses east of the sun then a crescent is seen in the early evening sky. By full moon the sun and moon are half a circle away (180º) and they appear opposite each other.[5]

As the moon begins to travel back towards the sun, then its waning phase takes place. But it also rises later at night. By the last quarter, the moon is highest in the sky a little before dawn and by the waning crescent it may rise only just before sunrise. The length of time that the moon can be seen in the sky also varies during its phases and at different times of the year. It is only at full moon that the moon rise and sunset coincide as do moonset and sunrise.

Therefore, it is quite usual to see the moon in the day sky – either in the evening in its beginning phases or in the morning at the end of its cycle. When the moon shows as a crescent it is often possible to see the rest of its shape glowing against the sky. This is because of earthshine – caused by sunlight being reflected back by the clouds around earth.[6] These are more of those 'once-you-know things', they're easily noticeable…

As I read, and then watch for myself, I become able to understand the moon's journey. One of the legacies of my residency is that I can now predict at what time and where in the sky I can expect to see the moon. I wonder at our (or at least my) glib acceptance that the moon just shows at night. It mystifies me how such a thing was missed from my education. I talk to friends and it appears the population is divided into those who are aware and those who aren't. And that also seems reflected in the poetry I read:

> The moon shuts its eye. Down in the street
> the same trolley is playing the pavestones.

For twenty-five years I've been waking
this way…

from **Waking** by Emma Jones[7]

Moon, worn thin to the width of a quill,
In the dawn clouds flying,
How good to go, light into light, and still
Giving light, dying

from **Moon's Ending** by Sara Teasdale[8]

I discover that the September moon was traditionally called the corn or barley moon, named because the brightness of the full moon gave farmers extra time to harvest their crops. Each full moon has a name.[9] Here are some of them:

MONTH	CELTIC	MEDIEVAL ENGLAND	ENGLISH
JANUARY	Quiet Moon	Wolf Moon	Old Moon
FEBRUARY	Moon of Ice	Storm Moon	Wolf Moon
MARCH	Moon of Winds	Chaste Moon	Lenten Moon
APRIL	Growing Moon	Seed Moon	Egg Moon
MAY	Bright Moon	Hare Moon	Milk Moon
JUNE	Moon of Horses	Dyan Moon	Flower Moon
JULY	Moon of Calming	Mead Moon	Hay Moon
AUGUST	Dispute Moon	Corn Moon	Grain Moon
SEPTEMBER	Singing Moon	Barley Moon	Fruit Moon

OCTOBER	Harvest Moon	Blood Moon	Harvest Moon
NOVEMBER	Dark Moon	Snow Moon	Hunter's Moon
DECEMBER	Cold Moon	Oak Moon	Oak Moon

And, of course, there is a blue moon.[10] When an extra full moon occurs within any of the seasons – four rather than the usual three – the third of the four is called a blue moon. This happens about seven times every nineteen years, so *once in a blue moon* is not as infrequent as you might expect.

There is romance in the names, alongside a grounding in the reality of times and seasons. I grew up in the era of the Apollo space missions when man was more interested in claiming rather than naming. I was only six when Neil Armstrong became the first man to walk on the moon and we didn't own a television, but his words: "That's one small step for (a) man, one giant leap for mankind," are immortalised in my mind. [11] I suspect it's the same for anyone who grew up through the 1960s and 70s. I still own a commemorative plate from that first moon walk. The flights to the moon brought an air of hope: if man could fly through space, exist in another place, then he could achieve anything using the wonders of science and technology. This hope was contradicted by the threats of nuclear war and the 'erection' of the Iron Curtain. But these also provided much of the spur for 'conquering' the moon as America and the USSR competed for supremacy.

The moon landings proved there was no Man in the Moon or indeed any life at all. Nor is it made of cheese, even if Wallace and Gromit did discover its cheesy delights on their *A Grand Day Out* in 1989.[12] It is an arid landscape with negligible atmosphere and much less gravity than on earth, hence the need for spacesuits with breathing apparatus and weights. Due to the lack of erosion the footprints made in Armstrong's giant leap will remain for millions of years.[13]

It is thought that the moon was formed about 4.5 billion years ago, when the earth was struck by some other planet – the 'Big Whack' theory.[14] Fragments flew off which eventually coalesced to make the moon. There's no water – what were originally thought to be lakes or seas, and thus named 'mares', were found to be craters caused by the impact of meteorites, asteroids and comets and subsequent flows of molten rock. Galileo was the first to try to map the moon using one of the earliest telescopes.[15] With increasingly powerful telescopes, orbiting satellites and the moon explorations themselves, the moon surface has now been extensively charted – most astronomy books give details and positions of the features on the surface of the moon we can see, such as the large basin of Mare Imbrium which spans 720 miles and the much smaller Aristarchus which is only 25 miles across.[16]

Has all this knowledge of the moon detracted from its literary or imaginative influence over us? Maybe; maybe not. In young adult fiction vampires have had a recent run of popularity and there's always a fascination about werewolves at full moon. Science and myth may overlap. With the forty year celebrations of the moon landing in 2009, a whole host of theories hit the Internet claiming we had been duped by an elaborate hoax.[17]

The moon has been connected with lunacy since the times of Aristotle and Pliny the Elder. Research projects are still undertaken by those anxious to prove or disprove some lunatic theory.[18] Lunacy is derived from lunar – another moon word. There has also been resurgence in interest of the moon's possible effects on women's menstrual cycles. Menses – a word connected to month and therefore moon. Such research fascinates me and I am swayed by some of the arguments, but unsure whether they supply the full picture.

But talking of pictures, I discover another feature of the moon – coronae. These are coloured concentric circles which appear around the moon when it is viewed through thin clouds. They can also be around the sun but because of the sun's glare it's more difficult to focus on them. Coronae are produced by the interference of light which has been diffracted around the outside of the water drops in clouds. The corona colours start as white in the middle (an aureole) to blue, green, yellow and red. These may be repeated in successive rings.[19] I never get to see a corona as clear as that – but I do see the more common form of a bluish aureole surrounded by a rust-coloured ring and I sometimes see two or three different colours. Though I read the scientific explanation for them, it doesn't detract from their enchantment or from being awed by such colours in nature.

Having had such a spectacular experience of sunset and moonrise on my first day at the hut, I wait with expectation for the next full moon, making sure that I am free to stay to see it rise. But the evening sky is thick with cloud: the sun sets behind them producing only a faint pink tinge to the western sky and the moon remains hidden. A good reminder that nature is not ours to command.

Of Crows, Gulls and Cormorants

To hatch a crow, a black rainbow
Bent in emptiness
Over emptiness
from ***Crow*** *by Ted Hughes* [1]

Ted Hughes' Crow is a powerful, devious bird intent on usurping God and the gods. In Australian aboriginal mythology, crow is a trickster character. Other traditions treat the crow as an omen of evil and death,[2] and a collective of crows is called a murder. Then there are scarecrows, eccentric dwellers of the British countryside.

In medieval times boys were employed as bird-scarers in fields newly planted with seed. They were given bags of stones or equipped with large wooden clappers. The Great Plague devastated the small-boy population so farmers, needing an alternative, created imitations from turnip heads and straw-stuffed clothes.

Scarecrows inhabited most seeded fields and though nowadays they are more often portrayed as friendly, harmless creatures, such as Worzel Gummidge or the brain-less scarecrow in the Wizard of Oz, they were originally meant to be fearsome deterrents of crows and rooks; birds considered such pests that Henry VIII put a bounty on each one.

Aware of some of this vilification, I sit by the side of my beach hut, in the autumn sunshine, watching a pair of crows. They hop and hunker along the slope pecking in the grass. These are carrion crows (*Corvus Corone)* – robust, black creatures – plumage, bill, legs and eyes are all black. One crow waddles and jumps all the way down the slope and onto the beach; then with a flap of its six-fingered wings lifts to perch on the groyne.

Over the coming days, I become more aware of the presence of this pair; they are far more frequent companions than any of my beach hut neighbours. In reality it is impossible to tell whether they are the same pair each time but, as crows are usually territorial, I suspect they could be; this hunch is backed by seeing similar pairings at various places on my walks. Crows generally mate for life so these may well have been a nesting pair. They brood between March and May and the young are fledged within four to five weeks, so by September any offspring would have left their parents.[3] I wonder where this pair might have nested – there is only a small patch of woodland near to the hut and I don't know whether the trees are suitable for a crow's nest.

The crows seem to prefer to be ground-bound as they search for food. To lift into the air, they arch and splay their wings – a movement which appears to involve considerable effort. They fly in short bursts, from pillar to post so to speak: from groyne to beach, from top of slope to further down. I recall the phrase 'as the crow flies' – the shortest distance between two points. This would seem to suggest that they are great, long-distance, straight-line fliers and I wonder if this is a feature of crows that I'm not seeing. It's not. I discover the phrase has been in print since 1758,[4] but it's inaccurate. Crows don't fly long distances and their path tends to be in large wheeling arcs.

Crows tend to be opportunistic scavengers, feeding on whatever they can find. They are happy to live in towns, raiding rubbish bins and picnic sites, as well as in the countryside. Shore-dwelling crows have developed a feeding technique which they share with gulls. At low tide, I watch them on the beach. A black 'stone' in its beak, a crow soars into the air, drops the 'stone' on to the shingle and swoops down after it. These are winkles and the fall cracks open the shell so the birds can feast on the flesh inside.

One day I walk eastwards. On an outcrop of shingle, I see a host of large black birds. I assume they must be rooks as they are known for their gregarious flocks. I take photos of them, hoping to add rooks to the list of birds I've seen during my residency but, on close examination, the photographs show that the birds lack rooks' feathered 'trousers'. As it is mid-October I decide they must be a post-breeding parcel, muster, or storytelling of crows.

Crows mingle on the shingle with the many gulls. The larger ones I recognise as herring gulls. These are common in Ramsgate and their loud *Kyow-kyow* has been my dawn chorus for over twenty years. Herring gulls have adapted well to man's invasion of their territory – they nest on chimney pots, pinch food from plates at seaside cafés and raid black bin sacks, scattering contents across the pavements. Thanet council recently introduced plastic canvas, gull-proof sacks for houses which are unsuitable for wheelie bins. I fully expect that the gulls will learn to penetrate them.

Herring gulls seem to inspire either love or hate. Many consider them a nuisance; I have a friend who calls them skyrats. But to me, an adult herring gull is a magnificent sight with its pure white head, neck and underside, silver-grey mantle and black wingtips. The colouring is so attractive that if it wasn't for the impressive yellow bill I'd be tempted to stroke one. So often they seem to soar in the air, not just to seek food, but for the pure hell of playing in the wind. They fly into the sunset, silhouettes against the colours of the evening sky.

I am reminded of *Jonathan Livingston Seagull* [5] and buy a copy to reread. It disappoints. Firstly, its title – I have been indoctrinated by a 'birding' friend that there are no such birds as seagulls, just different varieties of gulls. But the story also disappoints – I can't see any of the scared, food-obsessed birds that Richard Bach suggests is the norm. I guess, the ones I watch all must have come under Jonathan Livingston's influence and be flying free.

It takes four years for a herring gull to reach adulthood.[6] They are a bit ugly ducklingish with mottled brown feathers which are gradually replaced as they mature. The adolescents tend to gather in groups once they are fledged. At Tankerton, low tide reveals a couple of old tractor tyres in the muddy sand. These become playground toys for adolescent gulls as they squawk, squabble and jockey for position.

When my children were growing up there was an excellent museum in Dover called the *White Cliffs Experience*. Often on a wet school-holiday day we would take a trip there – they could use up energy climbing and exploring the wooden boat, experience an air-raid in a WWII street and be told the history of Dover by Captain Crusty the crab patrolling the beach with Sid Seagull and his nephew Pepe. These animatronic characters held my kids spellbound as they moved around the stage. Pepe was a typical adolescent herring gull, cheeky, daring, inquisitive and ready for adventure. Unfortunately, the museum has now closed; no longer considered viable.[7]

Adult herring gulls are typically solitary, coming together in their pairs to breed. But on the beach and slope near the hut, there are flocks of smaller gulls totalling much greater numbers than the herring gulls. These I don't recognise and so I head into Whitstable to Harbour Books.[8] It is a gem of a shop full of nooks and crannies stashed with good reads often significantly reduced in price. It's difficult for me to exit without having bought at least one book, often many more. This time is no exception: I purchase two collections of poetry, Paul Auster's *Man in the Dark* and the *AA Spotter Guide: Coastal Birds*.

Aided by the book I decide that the gulls are common gulls and eagerly draft a poem using my new knowledge. However, a couple of weeks later I dip into the guide again and realise that the birds don't have the yellow bills and legs of common gulls; they have red bills and legs. I search through the gulls listed and finally decide that they must be black-headed gulls. Why my mistake? Out of the breeding season, black-headed gulls don't have black heads. Instead their heads become white with dark smudges behind their eyes and so look quite similar in plumage to a common gull whose heads are specked with black. I redraft my poem. Actually, black-headed gulls never have black heads – their breeding plumage is a chocolate-brown cap. It makes you wonder how they got their names.

Their Latin name is more appropriate: *Lorus ridibundus* – the laughing gull. They can certainly create a raucous racket. In winter and summer, they have white neck and underside, grey wing feathers which show a white edge in flight and black tips to their primary feathers. They are considerably smaller than herring gulls but are actually our most common gull, inhabiting inland areas as well as coasts. Often, from my hut, I see flocks sitting on the water like a bevy of buoys and when the tide withdraws, they occupy the same position on the revealed beach.

Black-headed gulls aren't my only new bird discovery. At various points along the beach are drain-water run-off pipes. These outlets are marked by a post on which is mounted what looks like an upside-down, red, wooden laundry basket. Gulls often perch on these but they are also the haunts of another bird – a cormorant. This large black waterbird with broad wings has a powerful bill with a yellow base and hooked tip. Though it has webbed feet it can perch in trees (or on upturned laundry baskets). Cormorants are swimmers – they dive beneath the surface where they catch fish, particularly eels and flatfish.[9] After swimming, a cormorant preens its feathers with oil from a gland at the base of its tail and stretches out its wings to dry:

> You'd know her house by the drawn blinds –
> by the cormorants pitched on the boundary wall,
> the black crosses of their wings hung out to dry.
>
> from **At Roane Head** by Robin Robertson[10]

A cormorant is often perched on the basket near my hut when I arrive in the morning. I realise how easily I give it symbolism; correlate its presence with the lifting of my mood. As the lines from Robin Robertson's poem suggest it is a bird that evokes atmosphere. Its preen and stretch and low flight path over the sea are absorbing. I imagine there is only a solitary cormorant on this stretch of coast until one day, on my walk into Whitstable, I see two cormorants on two successive posts. Joy doubled. I also harbour the illusion that cormorants must be quite rare but my bird book tells me otherwise. And once I've learnt about them – guess what? I suddenly spot them elsewhere: in Ramsgate harbour, at Camden Lock, and on Dymchurch beach there's a family group – the three young having brown wings and a pale belly.

I'm entranced by cormorants. With astigmatism, I've always struggled to focus binoculars but I decide I will try again. I take a simple pair, a free gift on buying National Trust membership as a present for one of my daughters. They work. Or rather, I can see through them. Suddenly a whole new world comes into view – I can see not only the birds, but also out towards the horizon.

Aliens

Out towards the horizon white ladies whirr. A friend and I have nicknamed the wind turbines for their curvy shape and busy arms. When the sun shines they gleam, white and bright, but cloud-cover dulls them to grey spinsters. Often there's a mix of both ladies and spinsters. Using my new-found skill with binoculars I watch – they turn so the blades can catch the wind whose strength dictates the speed of whirr.

There are thirty ladies, all harnessing power for man, and from the shore they appear to be in a diagonal pattern: one lady, two, three, four, five, and back down again. But once I noticed them when I was flying from Manston to Edinburgh and from the air they are a rectangular block of six rows of five turbines. I draw a diagram of dots in my journal to work out how this can be. They are the Kentish Flats wind farm, erected in 2005 by Vattenfall. At that time, this was Britain's biggest wind farm with the largest turbines, set about 10 kilometres from the shore. The site is 10 square kilometres and each turbine is separated by 700 metres from its neighbour. The Vattenfall website states that rotor diameter is 90 metres and each blade weighs 6.6 tonne.[1] From this distance that's hard to envisage. Generated electricity is fed into a sub-station at Herne Bay. This wind farm was one of the first erected offshore in the Government's attempts to increase its renewable energy supplies. In 2008, the UK became the world leader in offshore wind power generation when it overtook Denmark.[2]

Wind turbines stir controversy. Vattenfall has also erected the Thanet farm off my local coast – a massive affair of 100 turbines which they claim could provide the electricity needs of 200,000 households. But energy generation is dependent upon wind strength: too weak and the turbines are idle; too strong and they must be switched off. Many say that the costs of erecting and maintaining sites, and of bringing the electricity to our homes, make them inefficient. Others claim turbines are an eyesore and they affect the environment, killing birds with their rotating blades. I think these white ladies are rather elegant and as they are far off I can't hear their moans and groans, often a criticism of onshore wind farms. I wonder if windmills caused a similar controversy when they were first constructed – monsters blotting the skyline; a necessary evil in the route to mechanisation. Nowadays we marvel at them and look to preserve the few remaining mills.

Guarding the ladies are hulking giants. At first I think they are boats but they are static and binoculars reveal some kind of tower structure. Walking through Whitstable harbour one day, I discover a notice that tells me about the Redsand Towers Sea Fort. That gives me enough information to have a good Google. And I discover a fascinating story. They were designed by an engineer, Guy

Maunsell, and so called Maunsell Towers. Maunsell was first commissioned by the Navy for defences that could house guns to shoot down enemy aircraft laying mines along the busy shipping lanes into the Port of London. Four were constructed and placed in the Thames Estuary in 1942. Only two remain – Knock John, abandoned off Shoeburyness and Roughs Tower off Harwich, now known as the *Principality of Sealand* which is occupied by 'Prince' Roy Bates and his family.

The Army decided they also needed forts to deter German aircraft from using the Thames as a navigational aid to find London. These are the ones I can see from my hut. Guy Maunsell was employed again and he designed a seven-tower fort: a control tower with predictors and radar, surrounded by four gun towers, a Bofors tower (named for the Bofors guns it housed) and a searchlight tower. They were constructed in Gravesend, towed down the estuary and lowered by hand-winch onto the seabed. And they are still there for me to see.

Actually, that's not quite true. Three army forts were placed in 1943 – Nore, Redsand and Shivering Sand – and all saw active service. They were maintained by a crew after the war until 1956. In 1953 the ship, *Baalback*, ran into the Nore Towers in fog, knocking over the Bofors Tower and a gun tower and killing four of the maintenance crew. This led to Nore being scrapped in 1959. Similarly, in 1963, the *Riberborg* crashed into one of the gun towers of Shivering Sand, so now it's left with six towers. Only Redsand is complete.

After the departure of maintenance crews, the forts lay abandoned but protected under the Official Secrets Act until 1995. That didn't stop invasion by pirates – of the radio kind. Spurred on by Radio Caroline, broadcasting from a boat in offshore waters, others took the initiative – 'Screaming' Lord Sutch occupied Shivering Sand and Radio 390 broadcast from Redsand. Prosecuted in 1966-7 the stations fell silent. The Admiralty removed access ladders and catwalks to make them more difficult to occupy.

Today Redsand has hopes for a renaissance. A dedicated team of enthusiasts is raising money and support to make the fort operational as a tourist attraction, as a radio studio, even as an unusual place for a wedding venue. An underwater structural survey revealed Redsand is still safe, so a new access system has been installed and restoration begun.[3]

East of the ladies another hulk sits. This dumpy dome structure looks black and lost. It's the seaward end of Herne Bay pier cut off from the shore after storms wreaked havoc in 1978 and 1979, leading to the pier being dismantled in 1980. This was the third pier built at Herne Bay, completed in 1899, a spectacular 1154 metres long – the second longest pier in England. It was constructed so passengers could disembark from steamers, the waters being too shallow for the boats to come nearer the shore. A railway ran along its length and there was a grand pavilion, complete with a rock maple floor, for roller skating, dancing and 'public events'.[4]

Fires and storms, popularity and misappropriation of funds, have all influenced the pier's history. During the Second World War, it was wrapped in barbed wire and women manufactured camouflage netting in its pavilion. In 1940 the army blew up two sections of the pier to prevent enemy landing, bridging the gaps with Bailey Bridges. It's been suggested that this was enough to weaken the pier leading to its eventual demise. The dome was deemed too solid for demolition, so remains isolated from the shore, protected by a solar-powered navigational light.

Weaving between and around all these aliens, boats ply their way up and down the Thames Estuary. I guess that their numbers are much reduced from even fifty years ago. Most seem to be container carriers – nothing special to look at. But at night they create their own magic – their warning lights join with those that protect the aliens, and a mysterious multi-coloured winking emanates from the darkened horizon.

Some boats don't voyage all the way to London and its surrounding docks; some stop at Sheppey. This island occupies the western horizon and has a boat-building tradition, with its associated industries, dating back to the time of Samuel Pepys. Nowadays it's better known for prisons and caravans. Though the island (or really three islands, Sheppey, Harty and Elmley) is only 36 square miles it houses three prisons and many more caravan parks. Sheppey is often the butt of jokes about being inhabited by alien people who all look the same due to generation after generation of inbreeding. This reputation isn't aided by the fact that during World War II all residents had to have a passport to be allowed on and off the island. Ostensibly this was because Sheppey acted as an offloading site for ammunition before boats travelled further up the Thames but…[5]

Sheppey is the only part of mainland Britain that's been conquered since William the Conqueror won the Battle of Hastings in 1066. A Dutch fleet sailed up the Thames Estuary, in June 1667, and captured the fort at Sheerness, the main town on Sheppey. They didn't seem to meet much resistance from underfed and underpaid men housed in an incomplete garrison. The Dutch overran the island, stayed a few days and left with supplies, ammunition and guns, burning everything else that they could.

The first time I visited Sheppey it was swathed in a thick hanging mist. As I drove over the Sheppey Crossing which rises above the Swale I could hardly see the cars in front and behind me, let alone the water under the bridge. It was an eerie experience. I've been back a couple of times but only to Sheerness. I still want to take myself to its southern edge and look towards Tankerton – reverse the view which I survey.

On a really clear day, beyond Sheppey, I can see the coast of Essex. From a map I work out that it is the area around Shoeburyness. But Essex makes a bigger impact: sometimes BOOMS shudder the air. These, I decide, must travel across the water from the MOD ranges situated on that part of the southern Essex coast.

Besides all these places and objects, alien and other, the horizon itself is fascinating. I read in *Colour and Light in Nature* that the horizon sky, during the day, is usually much brighter than sky at the zenith and it often appears white.[6] This is because when we look at the horizon our line-of-sight passes through so many air masses that the sky becomes almost opaque due to the multiple scatterings of the sunlight. This creates a sky as bright as it can be. This multiple scattering also causes the atmosphere to lose its blue colour. Zenith sky appears blue as it is 'thinner'. We see the sky as blue because blue, with the shortest wavelength of the colours, is least scattered. But when the atmosphere is 'thick', light photons scatter and re-scatter so many times that they get thoroughly mixed together and we see them as white.

Armed with this knowledge I keep a check on the horizon. Often the horizon sky is whitish even when up above the sky's a rich blue. But sometimes cloud cover causes the horizon to appear grey and at other times the colour seems to be more like that of the sea. I read more and discover that the horizon sky can become tinted by light reflected by the water.

And there are times when the horizon disappears. A haze descends and Sheppey, the Maunsell Towers and wind turbines are veiled from sight. Haze is caused by condensed water vapour or dust in the atmosphere. It's strange: sometimes I sit in beautiful sunshine by my hut but the horizon has vanished – one morning I arrive to find the ladies and the island lost but a lace-white moon hanging in the cloudless, blue sky above me; other days it is cloudy on the coast but out to sea the horizon is bright and clear. I record these conundrums in my journal as I try to capture the colour changes. And sometimes, when there is rain offshore but the sun shines behind me, I delight in spotting part or all of a rainbow perched on the horizon.

Defences

I look; morning to night I am never done looking.
Looking I mean not just standing around, but standing
around
as though with your arms open.

from **Where Does the Temple Begin, Where Does It End?** *by Mary Oliver* [1]

My attention turns from the horizon to the shore. Tankerton has a shingle beach. I would describe its pebbles as predominantly light brown though speckled with many other colours. When wet, after rain or when the tide has recently ebbed, they become brighter. One afternoon, feeling a bit lonely and not quite sure what to do with myself, I decide to investigate the stones. Armed with a notebook and artists' colour books,[2] I go down to the beach.

Aimlessly I finger pebbles, my back to a groyne and the sun on my face. But soon I'm scraping around, digging and delving, turning pebbles over and examining them individually, in their tens, in their hundreds… I become absorbed and start scribbling in my notebook:

> Pebbles on the beach – how to define them? They are each very different in shape, colour, texture – all they really share is solidity.
>
> No pebble is a single colour – even if you pick one up that appears to be, close examination reveals that you are wrong.
>
> Is a rounded shape instantly more aesthetically pleasing, more interesting, than an angular one?
>
> Some pebbles seem to have a thin outer layer of material and then a completely different core. Are others like that but I can't see their insides?
>
> Hidden among the stones are shells – some complete, some fractured and worn, but all with beautiful coloration.
>
> If you had to use one word you'd say that this shingle is brown. But it's not – there's black, grey and white, all intermingled in streaks, speckles and bands, and sometimes a bluish or pinkish tinge.

> And looking at the colour books, the 'brown' isn't brown at all – yellow ochre or raw sienna are more accurate colour descriptions.

Between moments of shingle exploration, I survey the sea, or watch walkers, joggers and cyclists on the promenade. I become rather philosophical and draft a twee poem about people and pebbles – no two exactly the same in shape or size or colour…

I'm not the only person who finds shingle fascinating. Toddlers delight in sorting, making piles or lining up stones on the path. They enjoy the clatter of a pebble dropping on to its companions or the plop of one thrown in the sea. And there are pebble 'experts', often a father-son combination, who select flat stones to send skimming over the water. Such simple pleasures. At dusk a treasure-seeker stalks the shingle, welly-booted and anoraked, ears muffed in headphones, metal detector in hand.

So many enjoy something that we rarely pause to think about. Our expectation is to see shingle on a beach, created over eons by the sea's erosion and deposition. I knew the groynes were planted on the shore but as I research Tankerton's coastal defences, I discover shifting shingle has also been a feature.

'Groyne' is a curious sounding word with perhaps connotations of groins or groans. I am intrigued about its origin but my dictionary definition is not particularly helpful: "groyne or esp US groin, n: a wall or jetty built out from a riverbank or seashore to control erosion. Also called spur, breakwater [C16 origin uncertain: perhaps altered from groin]." [3] Online I find explanations about the construction and purpose of groynes in protecting shallow coastlines but no further help about the word's derivation.

The groynes at Tankerton are made from wood – Ekki, a tropical hardwood. This was imported from a sustainable source in the Cameroon for a two phase upgrade, in 1999 and 2003, because the groynes were in poor condition, no longer retaining the shingle or protecting the sea wall. Ekki wood was chosen, rather than any British hardwood, because it is more resistant to marine borers and to erosion from shingle. An amazing 1275 cubic metres of wood were needed for the scheme, 13% of which was recycled from the old groynes. If all the timber was laid end to end it would create a line nearly 33 miles long. Altogether 1455 piles were driven into the ground and connected together with planks.

But repair of the coastal defences required more than new groynes. Some of the concrete sea wall needed to be reinforced and mended. And shingle was shipped in. It was dredged from the sea bed near Hastings and transported round the coast. As the shoreline at Tankerton is shallow, the stones were transferred from the dredger to flat-bottom barges which were then manoeuvred by tugs nearer the shore. Once the tide ebbed, a large shovel tipped the load onto the beach and bulldozers and excavators spread it. So imported shingle was mingled with the original and I have no way of knowing which pebbles are original and which are ones from the 130,000 cubic metres of added stones.[4]

The receding tide exposes sand. But this is not golden sand, great for castles and channels, such as on the beach at Ramsgate. This is a brown gloop that never dries out, decorated with occasional pebbles, seaweed and shells. When I walk through it wearing flip-flops, I squelch and stick, and splash mud up the back of my legs. The underlying geology is of London Clay rather than the chalk beds found just a few miles further along the coast.

London Clay is great for making bricks and for harbouring fossils but not for dry sand.

This geology provided a stone which birthed an Industrial Revolution here two hundred years before the coal, iron and steel industries of the north. In 1995, storms and heavy seas exposed timber frames set in yellow mortar on the Tankerton foreshore. Archaeological investigation identified these as part of the copperas workings dating to the late 16th and early 17th centuries. Copperas is nothing to do with copper. It is made from iron pyrites and is washed ashore, after erosion, in the form of knobbly twig-like fossils – the 'copperas stones'.

Copperas production probably began in Tankerton in 1588 when a Cornelius Stevenson first appears in the Whitstable parish records. He was a Dutchman, a Brabanter as they were known, who previously held a lease to work copperas in Dorset. Copperas stones were collected from the shore and placed in large troughs. Exposed to air and seawater, colonisation by bacteria and oxidisation occurred which after four years produced 'liquor' – dilute sulphuric acid and dissolved copperas. Poured into boilers with scrap iron the liquor was then concentrated.

This production marked the beginning of large-scale chemical manufacture. Copperas was used as a textile dye, to blacken leather, for writing ink, as eye ointment, to treat scab in sheep and as a cure-all for many ailments including as a laxative. Sulphur was also needed for 16th century gunpowder and finding a way to make this from copperas meant England was no longer reliant on importing sulphur from mines in Sicily – a great relief when relations with the Pope were not too healthy in Protestant England.[5]

There are records of a Whitstable copperas owner, in 1775, paying for a massive system of sea defences to protect the site from rising water levels, but by 1835 only one of six copperas buildings remained. As I study the shingle I wonder if copperas stones are still washed up and whether it is possible to recognise them. The romance of this first dangerous industry inspired a poem:

The Elizabethan Coast

In the year of our Lord 1588
Brabanter Stevenson fetched up,
promising rich pickings
to tempt us to work the copperas.
In Tankerton fish were our living
but I've no stomach for swell and squall.
I joined his gang, dug his pits,
collected the fossil twigs,
kept them bucked with seawater –
for a-four year!
                              That Brabanter paid well
and when he began to sell to wool
& leather men, engravers and quacks,
he was true to his word – our money grew.

But 'tis devil's brew! Tom slid a stone
in his pocket. By the time he were home
his gabardine were burned and holed.
And Harry, the fool, fell in the trough.
We fished him fast – but that night
he breathed his last.
                                    Aye, strange business!
The Dutchman, though, proved shrewd,

knew the worth of biding time,
shewed living as more than hand-to-mouth.

For those who didn't understand the science it must have seemed like magic for inert stones to produce such dangerous liquor. And that a stone could burn a hole in a pocket in a few hours must have made men wary of what they were handling. There are still industrial chemical works at some of the original sites of copperas production but not at Tankerton. But I do spot something that makes me think of alchemy: on a walk along the shore, one morning, I see an almost-perfect blood-red circle of shingle. From a distance, it looks as if somebody has transformed the stones. I approach with wonderment.

The reality, somewhat more mundane, is still awe-inspiring. In the centre of the circle are bits of charcoaled wood and other evidence of a fire. The red colouration appears to happen as stones split in the heat of the fire. Why do they turn red? I haven't been able to find out. But this splitting means building a fire directly on a shingle beach is potentially hazardous as stones can spontaneously fly out and cause injury; use of a fire pit or a raised barbecue are recommended.

I walk away from the circle. The phrase 'stony silence' slips into my mind; impassive, secret-keepers. But these stones aren't silent – every footstep creates a sound and they percuss and rattle with each incoming tide.

Tide and Time Wait for No Man

John Banville begins *The Sea,* by describing an unusually high tide:

> All morning under a milky sky the waters in the bay had swelled and swelled, rising to unheard-of heights, the small waves creeping over parched sand that for years had known no wetting…[1]

The opening details unnerving phenomena and twice the narrator says "I would not swim again" after that day. By conveying the disturbing tide Banville conjures the story's suspense.

I know the sea is dangerous. The tsunami on Boxing Day, 2004, caused by an earthquake in the Indian Ocean, dramatically showed its devastating potential. Plugging the phrase 'Deaths at Sea' into the Internet brings more evidence – from merchant seamen to P&O Cruises, from wartime to gas and oil rigs. Many have lost their lives at sea. But I've never been affected by such tragedy, so as I sit watching waves gently lap on a sunny September day, it's hard to imagine that on 31st January 1953, the night's high tide flooded Whitstable.

Seawater breached the partly completed new sea wall at Horsebridge, the harbour and along Beach Walk. Oyster barrels were swept away and found floating along the High Street. The old reservoir and drainage systems were insufficient to cope, so overflowed, burst, and flooded further areas. On the golf course the water rose to the height of the clubhouse roof. Beach huts were destroyed and other buildings badly damaged. Many shops had to trade from top floor rooms until the water receded and their premises could be cleaned and renovated.[2]

But difficult for me to imagine, even after watching TV footage of recent floods in other areas of the country. Unless you've been there, felt its rage… For most of my residency the tide's ebb and flow seem quiet and unassuming, with barely a white horse out to sea or a surge and crash on the shore. I have to remind myself that the groynes and the sea wall are there for good reason.

September and October 2011 are unseasonably mild, so it's also difficult to imagine the sea freezing over. I was born in March 1963 and my mother would occasionally hint about the hard time she had carrying me that winter. But I hadn't really understood why. The winter of 1962/3 was one of the coldest on record. The Internet provides pictures of fishing boats trapped in Whitstable harbour, ripples and waves frozen in time and snow covering the beach.[3] Consistent temperatures of under –2°C are required for the sea to turn to ice as salt lowers the freezing point. I now have much more sympathy for my mother who, pregnant with her fourth child and living in Lancashire, experienced sixty-six consecutive days and nights with temperatures below freezing.[4]

The residency is an unsettling time as I try to form thoughts and write. I'm aware that my relationship to place is shifting, alongside the desire to understand more of the nature of this particular location. The restlessness of the water, the constant churn, can feed into my feelings. Sometimes its lap plays *soothing, soothing* and I become lulled, but at other times the insistent rattle of shingle forces me to pay attention.

> …But the sea revises itself over and over. When
> he arose in the morning or looked at it at night, it
> was always a new version of it.
>
> from **The Echoes Return Slow** by R.S.Thomas [5]

But the tides also feed the mathematical side of my character and I become fascinated with tide times and the progression of the tide through time. I print off timetables from the Canterbury City Council website[6] and pin them up in the beach hut. One day a nurse rushes past as I sit on the grass. She makes some comment about the lovely weather and wondering whether the tides will be suitable for her to swim at the weekend. I dash into my hut and tell her the high tide times for the next few days. That is satisfying.

Another trip to Harbour Books and I buy *The Wavewatcher's Companion* by Gavin Pretor-Piney. Better known for cloud-spotting he became absorbed by waves breaking on the rocks in Cornwall. The book's chapters each describe a different wave – from sea to sound, from speech to colour.

The seventh chapter is about tides and Pretor-Piney takes great delight in informing that he could win any pub quiz with his answer to the question: which is the biggest wave? They are not the breakers that crash onshore in hurricanes, nor even tsunami. The largest waves are the tidal movements of the oceans – tide waves – which may have an amplitude (height from peak to trough) of a only few feet but can have wavelengths of several hundred miles.[7]

How are they formed? It's mainly to do with the moon and sun's gravitational pulls. Isaac Newton – he of the apple falling on head fame – was the first to attempt an explanation of tides as a consequence of the gravitational effects of celestial bodies. Though the sun is a larger body and therefore has a bigger gravitational pull, its influence is less because the moon is much nearer to Earth. Newton's Universal Law of Gravity states: the gravitational force exerted by a body decreases in proportion to the inverse square of the distance from that body. Using a squared scale rather than a linear one means that effects diminish more quickly.

Gravitational pull causes the waters of the earth to bulge in the regions closest to the body exerting that pull. Both the sun and moon exert their influence so the biggest effect is found when they are aligned. Because of the earth and moon's rotations this occurs when we see a new or full moon; then high tides are high and low tides are low. These, rather confusingly as they happen all year round, are called spring tides. The opposite of these are neap tides when variation is much less. This happens when the sun and moon are separated by 90° in relation to the earth.[8]

All around the coast of Britain we experience two high tides and two low tides every day – well, almost every day. Because the moon's rotation is not actually synchronised with what we call days and months, the timing of the tides progresses. So, high and low tides arrive later each day and every so often there may only be one high tide or low tide in what we call a day as the next one slips into the following twenty-four hour period.

Two high and low tides is called semi-diurnal and is common on the Atlantic coasts of the United States and the coastline of Europe. Other areas of the world, such as parts of the Gulf of Mexico and Southeast Asia, only experience one high and one low tide a day – a diurnal tide. The west coast of Canada and the United States experience mixed tides when successive high-waters and low-waters differ considerably, so they have a higher high water and a lower high water as well as a lower low water and higher low water each day.[9]

The actual timing of high tides and low tides is also affected by local coastline factors. That is why tide times vary along each particular stretch of coast. The range of the tides varies with the closeness of the sun and moon to Earth so at different times of the year we see variety in tide heights. Local geography also influences, as does the size of the water body. Places on large ocean coastlines see greater variety in tidal range than those on smaller seas.

A tale is told that Alexander the Great, who only knew about the Mediterranean's small tidal range, was on his way to conquer the Indian subcontinent when he moored on the river Indus. He was totally surprised when a few hours later his boats became stuck in the mud. Worse was to come – the mouth of the Indus acts as a funnel and the returning tide re-enters as a bore of rushing water. Alexander's boats were pulled from their moorings and smashed against the river banks.[10]

I was once informed by a lady who regularly sails that there is a time when the positioning of the water is stationary. This is known as slack water and occurs for about 20 minutes at the turning of the tide and can be associated with the wind dropping or changing direction, or with bird life becoming quiet.[11]

I find identifying slack tide difficult. But something I do observe puzzles me as it doesn't match up with what I have been reading. At Tankerton the biggest variation in the high and low tides occurs a couple of days after new and full moon. My observation is backed up by the local tide timetables. Surely this is wrong? All the books and websites in my research suggest that it should be at new or full moon? Finally the often-maligned Wikipedia provides a satisfactory explanation:

> The tidal forces due to the Moon and Sun generate very long waves which travel all around the ocean following the paths shown in co-tidal charts. The time when the crest of the wave reaches a port then gives the time of high water at the port. The time taken for the wave to travel around the ocean also means that there is a delay between the phases the moon and their effect on the tide. Springs and neaps in the North Sea, for example, are two days behind the new/full moon and first/third quarter moon. This is called the tide's age.[12]

Height and force of tides are affected by weather conditions; thus prevailing winds can cause tides to rise much higher than would be predicted by the gravitational forces alone. One day I see a billowing effect – the direction of the wind is interacting with the incoming tide and this causes the waves to look like they are piling up and falling over each other rather than coming into the shore. Actually the incoming tide here flows from east to west and the outgoing from west to east – parallel to the shore – so even either side of a groyne the water appears at different levels.[13]

Constant variation of water levels means animals and plants living in intertidal zones have to be able to shift with the tide or cope with alternately being submerged in water and then exposed to air. The daily tides also cause erosion and deposition resulting in a constantly changing coastline.

The Street

Tankerton has its own version of Atlantis. At low tide 'The Street', appears. The story is told that once long ago, when minstrels, peddlers, tumblers and jugglers roamed the country, this spit would lead them to a thriving village; some called it Graystone and others Le Craston. They would always be welcome to entertain or sell their wares. Until one stormy night the village disappeared – the houses and church, the people and dogs, the horses and goats and the three-legged cat were all swept into the sea, never to be seen again. But it's said if you listen on a balmy breeze, you can hear bantering villagers about their business and smell on the night air the smoke from their fires. (Or possibly, teenagers late-night barbecuing.)

Well, that's something of an exaggeration of the story. And in reality, there's no evidence for the presence of the village other than fragments of tile and other building debris that are sometimes washed up on the shore. Nor is there any evidence for another theory that the spit was once a Roman causeway for loading and unloading cargo.[1] But it does appear to be a place of pilgrimage. Every low tide people walk along it, with or without their dogs. When my daughter and her friend visit from Hertfordshire, arriving at low tide, they immediately feel called to walk the Street. People share the spit with the gulls using the shingle for their shellfish bombing missions. Unlike Long Rock, a shingle shelf further east, the Street is not a good place for fossil hunting. It seems people walk just because they can.

And so, of course, do I. Not every day but often. The amount of spit exposed varies with the lowness of the low tide. Sometimes there's only a shortish, roughly rectangular protuberance, at other times it becomes sinuous, stretching and snaking into the water. I choose to explore one day shortly after the new moon when I know that it will be a low, low tide. I wear flip-flops so there's no need for me to worry about negotiating surface water and I stride out from the beach. The spit runs perpendicular to the shore and once beyond a small amount of gloopy sand, it is composed of shingle. Eyes towards the ground I spot the occasional starfish, stranded seaweed with standfasts exposed and shells scattered on and among the shingle. I look up and enjoy the patterns of the water as it plays around the spit.

I keep walking, following the receding tide right to the spit's tip. But is it? There's no way of really knowing how far the spit continues beyond the low water mark. I am adopted by a spaniel with a tennis ball who I try to ignore but his baleful eyes and eagerness to play win me over. I join in his game and throw the ball into the sea for him to retrieve. He is in the company of two lanky lads in long shorts. They have stripped off trainers and socks and are gleefully wading into the shallows in an attempt to outpace the tide.

This far out the spit begins to curve towards the east. The beach huts on the shore look more like dolls' houses and people walking the promenade become Lowry 'matchstalk men'. The spit itself is divided, colour wise, into two halves along its length. The western half (left hand side as you walk out) is predominantly the burnt ochre/raw sienna of the shingle on the beach. But the eastern side appears as a deeper greeny-grey colour. I stoop to examine this difference and discover that the stones on this side of the spit have tiny barnacles clinging to their upper surface; tens, even hundreds on each stone. Most are only a couple of millimetres in diameter, a few are maybe one centimetre across. They give the stones the grey appearance and beneath them each pebble is tinged green. I can't tell if this colouration is due to weathering or because of some substance secreted by the barnacles. I walk back to the east side and find a few stones that are barnacled but most are clear of accretions.

Retired geography teacher, Martin Knight, explains on his website about this colour contrast:

> there is a clear contrast between the steeper, newer shingle on the west side and that on the east, reflecting recent dominance of estuary currents and wave action over North Sea coastwise drift. Note the flat top, and the shape of the stones: smaller, more rounded and more uniform than on the beaches, suggesting long-continued low energy wave action in a shallow environment.[2]

The barnacles have had time to grow on the older stones. The spit also affects wave action. Those waves coming in on the west side are full of energy and drive. East, all is gentleness and ripples.

At October full moon I am on the spit with a friend at evening low tide. We watch a rather indifferent sunset and are disappointed to find cloud cover so thick that the moon can't even peep out. But we decide to walk anyway. We are not alone – others feel the need for pilgrimage too. But it is a disorientating experience. Though I know it is safe underfoot, as we go further from the shore and dusk darkens to night, everything become less familiar. I wonder whether I am going to splash into some unknown hole or trip on some boulder. Warnings about the dangers of being on the spit at tide-turn flash into my head. What has always been a simple pleasure suddenly feels much more of an adventure. It is on this night that, as we turn to head back for the shore, unsure of our footing any longer, we are greeted by the Halloween mask of Beacon House, small in the distance but seemingly aflame.

There are some who walk the spit when it is not low tide. Michaelmas Day is a gloriously sunny day. I am in my hut, busily noting the colours of the sea and sky when I look up to a strange sight: a man, golden-haired and tanned skin, with bright yellow top and green bag, has appeared like a sea-god risen from the waves. I dash out from my hut, binoculars in hand, to get a better look. He stands with a fishing rod in his hands, right out at sea, but only thigh-deep in the water. I suddenly realise – he is walking the spit wearing leg-length waders and therefore able to get much further out into the sea, but avoid the sucking sand. How a little local knowledge helps. Still, he is a sight to behold standing in the pastel-blue water, casting his line, and though I see other fishermen using the same technique on other days, none can quite catch my attention like that first apparition.

Spits are formed by Longshore Drift. What a great name for a roving sailor. 'Have you heard the story of Longshore Drift? One fine day in 1566, he set sail from Whitstable on the *Oyster Rose* for the distant horizon, never to return to shore. But the tale is told, that down through the years *Oyster Rose* appears, sometimes in the Mediterranean, sometimes in the Caribbean, Atlantic or Pacific and once way down in the Antarctic Sea, and the voice of Longshore drifts over the water singing shanties of his Nancy and his North Kent home.'

Actually, longshore drift is the movement of material along a coast by waves which approach at an angle to the shore but recede directly away from it. The material is moved in a zigzag pattern in the direction that the waves hit the beach. But if the angle of the coast suddenly turns a spit can begin to form. This creates a barrier so more material collects on the spit and it becomes longer which then creates a bigger barrier and more material collects which then… The spit also provides shelter so mud or salt flats can build up around it.[3]

In researching longshore drift, I discover that a spit can also be called a shoal. This is a new meaning of the word for me – I have always associated shoal with a group of fish. But a spit or shoal which has developed from the deposition of granular material also causes localised shallowing or shoaling of the water.[4]

One day I walk back along the spit ahead of the returning tide. It's definitely a feature of this coastline that stirs the imagination. It may never have led to a lost village nor been used by Roman conquerors. But as I reach the divide between spit and shore I spot something that tells of another invasion.

Cockles and Mussels Alive and Dead

Half hidden in the muddy sand revealed at low tide are, what appear to be, fossilised knuckles and vertebrae of ancient sea monsters. Their curved contours are brown, cream and pinkish tinged; remains from eons ago when mythical creatures swam the seas and sheltered on the North Kent shore.

In fact, these are much more recent invaders, unintentionally brought from America in 1887 to the Essex coast. Overfished oyster beds needed new supplies and some bright spark thought it would be a good idea to import stock. Slipper limpets cadged a ride and finding conditions satisfactory, multiplied, causing the oysters' further demise. Slipper limpets are not predators but they thrive in the same conditions that oysters need and therefore compete with them. On the British coast – slipper limpets have won.[1]

But why do they look like knuckles or vertebrae? They share the same habit as the common limpet, so often found with its cone stuck tightly to sea walls and old boats. The slipper limpet also attaches to a surface but unlike the common one, they congregate one on top of the other. The collective name for slipper limpets is a bungalow which I find rather curious as they never exist as a single storey.

Slipper limpets belong to the snail family but their shells are not typically snail-like. The opening is enlarged and widened so the shell looks more like an upturned boat than the usual snail's house. A flat shelf projects halfway across the opening and the only trace of a snail-shell's coils is a round knob at one end. Slipper limpets reproduce by internal fertilisation but because they can't move around they need to live close, literally on top of each other, for fertilisation to occur.

Chains of limpets form with the lowest limpet clinging to a stone or empty shell. This lowest limpet is female and the ones on top of her develop as males. When mating, a male extends his extra-long penis down the side of the shells and inserts it into the bottom female. She lays her eggs and attaches them underneath her to the same stone or shell, providing protection until they hatch. A baby larva swims to find a stack of slipper limpets, fastens itself to the top and matures as a male If a baby doesn't find other limpets, it adheres to a rock, develops as a female and excretes a chemical to attract other larvae and so a new chain begins. Slipper limpets can live for several years but eventually the old female dies. The next slipper limpet in the chain continues to hang onto the empty shell and transforms to become the matriarch.[2]

With these habits slipper limpets quickly multiply, smothering and starving their oyster neighbours. They can cover the clean shells needed by settling oyster spat. Their larvae drift on currents and so populate new areas. The result – in less than 130 years, slipper

conditions are right, periwinkles will spawn many times through a year.[7]

In my shingle sifting I discover many empty shells amongst the stones: slipper limpets, winkles and cockles, and a few whorling, ridged, dull yellow snail-like shells. Some of these are eroded revealing a porcelain-white inner surface with an elegant inner pillar. They belonged to whelks and the empty shells are a popular home for hermit crabs – a fact used as an effective metaphor by Arthur Conan Doyle:

> She can project herself into my body and take command of it. She has a parasite soul; yes, she is a parasite, a monstrous parasite. She creeps into my frame as the hermit crab does into the whelk's shell. I am powerless. What can I do? I am dealing with forces of which I know nothing.
>
> from **The Parasite**[8]

Whelks aren't often seen alive on the shore. They can't cope with low salinity so tend to live beyond the low tide mark. They move by gliding along secreting slime. If alarmed, they withdraw into their shell, sealing the entrance with a shelly plate at the end of their tail.

Whelks eat most things, detecting prey by smells carried in the water. They feed on worms and carrion and will drill through oyster and cockle shells to scrape out the flesh. They have a special accessory boring organ which secretes shell-dissolving chemicals, and a radula, whose rough end is used for the scraping and which is situated, with the whelk's mouth, at the end of a long proboscis.

Though whelks are infrequently spotted, their egg cases are commonly washed up. Whelks lay eggs between November and

January. The female secretes yellowish capsules which stick to stones and to each other. A female lays several layers, over a number of days, to make a mass about the same size as herself. Each capsule contains hundreds of eggs, but only a few are fertilised. This means that when the baby whelk hatches it has a readymade food supply. They emerge from the capsule in the spring and this is when the empty egg cases arrive on the beach looking like dried up balls of popcorn.[9]

Whelk capsules are not the only egg cases washed up. Mermaid's purses are the empty cases of sharks, rays and dogfish. Shark and ray cases are generally dark brown or black, almost square in shape and with tendrils at each corner which attached the egg case to seaweed. Shark and ray purses are easier to find on this stretch of coast than those of the dogfish which are a lighter brown and more rectangular. All are usually empty – mermaids don't have much spare cash.[10]

I walk along the shore in one direction or the other on most days of my residency. Sometimes I have a definite purpose; mostly I wander, browse and delve. Each time there are new revelations which I try to assimilate. I'm observing colour and writing poems, but there is so much... One day, at very low tide, I see small circular dints in the sand. It is only when I chance upon a razor shell not completely submerged that I twig as to the reason for the dints. And there are scallops, cuttlefish, top shells, wedge shells and tellins waiting to be discovered.

This wealth leads me to compose a shellfish blessing:

Blessing

May the road you walk be edged with scallops.
May you be kept from poverty's pincers.
May you winkle out from stormy waters,
all your whelks heal without a scar.
And until we meet again
may God grow your grit within an oyster shell.

Yes, there's more: for Whitstable is famous for oysters.

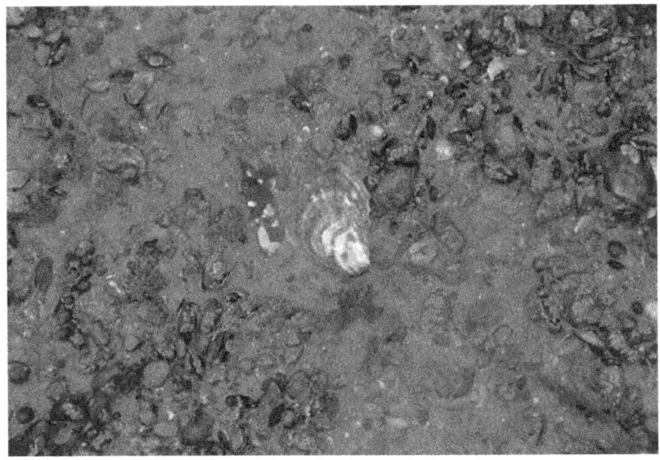

The World's Mine Oyster…

…says Pistol to Falstaff in *The Merry Wives of Windsor*[1] when Falstaff refuses to lend him a penny. And so Shakespeare invented or popularised a phrase that made oysters synonymous with opportunity. Well, for the fishermen of Whitstable their 'land' of opportunity sat on their doorstep.

The Romans, once they'd finished conquering, settled and indulged an enthusiasm for shellfish. Remains are found at Roman sites all over Britain. Oysters were exported to Rome and the waters around Whitstable provided a plentiful supply. So maybe the rumours are true: the Street was a causeway built to speed shipment of this aphrodisiac.

Through the centuries, our appetite for oysters has risen and fallen. In medieval times, the church inflicted fish days for fasting and, according to the medical profession of the time, meat and fish should be eaten separately. By the seventeenth century fashions had changed and oysters were stuffed into turkeys or poured over capon and ducks.[2] This, of course, was rich folks' feasting. But oysters, particularly pickled, became food for the Victorian masses – so much so, that Charles Dickens in *The Pickwick Papers* has Sam Weller say: "Poverty and oysters always seem to go together."

Ostrea edulis – edible oysters – are the only species native to British waters. They are bivalves with rough, scaly shells which are a yellowish-grey colour. The lower concave shell is fixed by the oyster to an underwater surface. The upper shell is much flatter and fits inside the lower one. They are roughly pear-shaped and though ugly on the outside, they hide a smooth, glossy, mother-of-pearl interior.[3]

Adult oysters spend their life on the seabed where they pump water through a gill-chamber collecting algae for food. They take about four years to reach maturity and then alternate between being male and female. First, they produce sperm, then eggs, then sperm again. When one male releases its sperm into the water, this acts as a trigger for the others. Sperm are drawn into the female through their filtering system and eggs are fertilised internally. How the females differentiate between algae and sperm is a trifle mind-boggling. Little larvae hatch and stay in the mother until they are about 0.2mm. On release, they swim around for two weeks feeding on plankton before settling to the bottom to search for a suitable place to live. They prefer being near other oysters to give them a greater chance of taking part in the fertilisation game; and they like somewhere clean – old shells being a great choice. The larvae, known as spat, cement themselves to their chosen spot and become tiny oysters about the size of a pinhead.[4]

Oysters will grow out at sea but are often found in shallow estuaries. In *Through the Looking Glass,* Tweedledee entertains Alice with *The Walrus and the Carpenter.* It must have been low tide when the baby oysters were persuaded for: "A pleasant walk, a pleasant talk,/ Along the briny beach," only to find they were to be seasoned with pepper and vinegar, and eaten with a loaf of bread for supper.

Popularity and cheapness were the oysters' downfall. They became overfished, even though companies developed systems of breeding and stocking company beds. Portuguese and American species were imported as seed oysters. Unfortunately, they are slow to breed in our colder waters but their competitors and predators who hitched a ride – the slipper limpets and the American Oyster Drill – aren't. A supposed solution compounded the problem.

But for many centuries oyster fishing was big business in Whitstable. The website, *Simply Whitstable*[5] holds a treasure trove of stories about the local oystermen and the companies they served – the Whitstable Oyster Company (dating back to the 1400s), the Seasalter and Ham Oyster Fishery Company (formed in 1893) and the Faversham Oyster Fishery Company (probably originating in the 1100s). They employed dredgermen, or drudgermen as they were known locally, to dredge (drudge) up oysters. The men sailed yawls – typically a yawl is a double-masted boat but others were adapted, and a single-masted, straight-bowed, counter-sterned boat has become iconic of the oyster yawls or smacks of Whitstable. These were moored at sea because of the shallow coastal waters and the men would row out to them in tenders. They were Day Fishermen – working with the tide, they set out a little later each day.

A typical crew consisted of four men and each would work one to three dredges. It was heavy demanding work. The dredges were made of an iron A-frame with a netted back and a metal chain-link bottom and they were pulled along the seabed to lift the oysters.

Not only oysters were trapped – other fish and stones could weigh down the dredge as it was pulled back into the boat.

The men were in charge of making and maintaining their own dredges using frames created at the local forge. Boats would be overhauled in the summer months when oysters were spawning – never eat oysters in a month without an R. But the beds would still have to be checked for predatory starfish which, when caught, were sold to farmers for fertiliser. They also fished for cockles and whelks or, if times were tough, dredged for stones to be used in concrete.

The companies owned the waters around Whitstable and their processing sheds lined the shore. But the waters in front of the Little Blue Hut were the preserve of the Flatsmen. The Kentish Flats, east of The Street, were considered common ground and were spawning sites for native oysters. The 'freelance' Flatsmen dredged for both mature and immature oysters. The mature ones they sold privately for eating, but immature oysters were sold to the companies to stock the company beds.

The last remaining yawl with a permanent home in Whitstable is the *Favourite*[6] which is located between two houses on Island Wall – in sight of the sea but no longer seafaring. However, the Whitstable Oyster Company still exists, with its buildings at Horsebridge converted into a seafood restaurant. The waters are owned by the Company – so Whitstable is one of a few places where the shore and sea are private. The Company, from its lowest ebb in 1978, has rebuilt the business and invested in the oyster beds. Outside the restaurant are heaped-up trays of empty shells. Signs request: *Please Don't Take. Oyster Shell Recycling. Re-establishing oyster beds.* The Company has also diversified, incorporating other restaurants, a hotel and a brewery into their business and converting some of the old fishermen's huts into unique cottages for holiday makers.[7]

The 1980s saw another revival with the resurrection of the Whitstable Oyster Festival.[8] This dates back to Norman times as an annual thanksgiving for the oysters and for the survival of the drudgermen. A 'holy day', it included a church service followed by games, dancing, competitions and, of course, feasting. But not oysters. It took place in July (No R), traditionally a quieter time for oystermen who couldn't afford to lose a day's fishing in the season. Nowadays it's a week-long festival, not only celebrating oysters, but the many aspects of Whitstable's thriving business and cultural life. There is a symbolic landing of oysters by the Sea Scouts and a Blessing of the Waters, alongside arts and family events.

The festival is long gone by the time I start my residency, but in the Little Blue Hut hangs a photo of a blazing grotter – the work of a previous resident. The flames seem to flicker and dart from the picture. Grotters are hollow mounds of sand and mud which are decorated with oyster shells. Children beg a 'penny for the grotter' in a local twist on the Guy Fawkes tradition. They remain part of the new Oyster Festival though more often lit by candles than set ablaze. A tamer time perhaps?

Oyster fishing is no longer big business here, but Whitstable harbour still seems to thrive with boats and fish, stalls and markets. It's a joy to explore.

An Aggregate Harbour

Whitstable harbour is an interesting mix of fishing and frivolity, leisure and industry. I walk from my hut along the promenade past the Hotel Continental and the back of the Leisure Centre. The skyline is dominated by a corrugated-metal clad tower and its accompanying silver-pole chimney. Lower buildings are similarly clothed and there's also a couple of dumpy 'silos'. The site is fenced by old railway sleepers: not a pretty sight. In the harbour, most of the east quay is a depositary for pyramids of gravel, which are sprayed by water from hose-pipes and kept in check by more railway sleeper fences.

Unattractive, maybe, but important for the harbour's vitality. They belong to Brett Aggregates[1] which has been associated with the harbour for almost 80 years. Famous for production of tarmacadam for Kent roads, the company still imports stones and the plant manufactures asphalt. Their rent to the council accounts for about 60% of the harbour income.

Whitstable harbour was built in the 1830s by a railway company. The Canterbury and Whitstable Railway, locally known as the Crab and Winkle Line, was the first railway to transport passengers under steam power using Stephenson's *Invicta*. That's not strictly true. *Invicta* couldn't manage to pull the carriages up the hilly parts of the seven miles between Canterbury and Whitstable and so stationary steam-engines were placed at strategic points to winch the train. The Railway wanted a harbour for importing goods and also to connect passengers with London via steamship. 10,000 people attended the official opening in 1832.

The opening of the North Kent Railway later in the century and the improvement of roads were the eventual death knell for this little line. It closed to passengers in 1932. The harbour remained active with fishing boats and for importing coal, grain and timber. During WWII munitions were landed. But when British Rail finally deserted the railway line in 1952, the harbour fell into disrepair, only sustained by local enthusiasts. Whitstable District Council bought it in 1958 for £12,500. Nowadays the harbour is run by a Harbour Board under the auspices of Canterbury City Council and the path of the railway line has become the Crab and Winkle cycle route.[2]

Enough facts and figures – more interesting to tell of Dead Man's Corner where a body washes up on each spring tide and tormented spirits howl on stormy nights. Well, maybe not, but tradition claims that this corner, between the east and south quays, is the place where lost souls surface.

In reality, you are far more likely to see ordinary flotsam and jetsam or weed, plastic bottles, oil patterns and grime, rather than any human remains. At Dead Man's Corner the trains were loaded and unloaded. Now it is home to a decking stage with a back wall of steel mesh baskets filled with pebbles; a regeneration project, it's made from materials that represent the harbour's history and provides free seating and a potential place for entertainments.[3]

Nearby is another renovation. Whitstable Harbour Village looks like a congregation of old fisherman's huts, in keeping with the bigger dark wood-clad buildings on the western quay. But it's a modern incarnation. In 2007 a small market began which has become home to many local entrepreneurs selling arts, crafts, food and kite-flying fun. The huts fill up part of the south quay and as I walk past, stallholders are enticing the crowds, brought by the good weather, with eye-catching wares and myriad scents and spices which mingle with the expected fishy smells.[4]

The south quay seems the place for reinvention. A few days previously I'd watched a sailing boat off the coast. Single masted, her russet, canvas sails stood out against the sky. She looked sturdy and majestic, hinting of a long gone era and I'd wondered about the boat's origins. And here she is, moored to the quay: *Greta*, a Thames sailing barge. Built in 1892 in Essex, she transported grain, malt and building products up the Thames estuary. She was used by the Ministry of Supply in WWII to take ammunition from Rochester to naval vessels anchored nearby and was one of the hundreds of small boats that helped with the evacuation at Dunkirk in 1940. Greta has the honour of being the oldest active Dunkirk Little Ship.[5]

And she is active – over a hundred years since her creation Greta still sails. For those who want a close-up view of the white ladies and the Maunsell giants or wish to try to spot seals off the coast of Sheppey, then Greta provides a glamorous day trip. I pick up a leaflet and ponder embarking. Memories surface of feeling wretchedly seasick whilst whale-watching on a small boat off the coast of South Africa. I decide I'll just enjoy the sight of the boat in harbour and its glorious vision from afar.

Greta seems much grander than the other moored boats. These are working boats too – for fishing. I watch as a mechanical 'hand' scoops from a boat's hold. It comes out dripping seawater and sometimes dangling seaweed but always with its claw full of shellfish. I wander round onto the much newer west quay (photos on the Internet of the frozen sea of 1963 show no west quay). The hand is unloading cockles but there are also whelks piled into large plastic tubs. West Whelks dates back to the 1800s and Derek West, the 'Whelkman', has been working in the business for over 65 years. Now in his eighties he no longer fishes but he and his wife still winkle out whelks from their shells ready for sale.[6]

West Whelks, Whitstable Fish Market, Wee Willie Winkle's Kitchen, the Crab and Winkle Restaurant and other outlets provide for anyone wanting the full fishy experience. Orange, turquoise and beige nets cascade out from plastic tubs, over chain-link fences and onto the ground, and thick ropes are coiled around mooring posts which I can't help noticing are like white sculptures of ladies' busts. At low tide, the harbour almost empties of water and the fishing boats seem 'stuck in the mud'. But as the tide flows the boats rise up alongside the harbour walls until they are ready to go to sea once more. All are brightly coloured with interesting names – Boy Callum and Charlie Boy – not the usual ladies. Gulls squabble on the cockle pyramid and round by the West Whelks building, adolescent gulls peck at a bowl of grain alongside a duck.

Or at least I think it is a duck. It's not the usual mallard, some of which reside in Ramsgate harbour. It's quite large for a duck, with mainly chestnut brown feathers but has a white neck and breast. It has yellow feet and a bright red bill. It's also red around its eyes. This time I have my camera with me so I take photos to help with its identification. But when I get back to the hut, I'm stumped. It doesn't appear to be any of the ducks in my bird books. I resort to sending an email to a friend with the photo attached to ask for her 'bird expert' husband's help in solving the mystery. His reply:

> This is a domesticated type of duck. It is (mostly) Muscovy duck but a variety that has altered its colour a bit. Muscovy ducks are found in the wild in South America and have been domesticated by the Indians because they are good egg-layers in captivity.[7]

This duck in the harbour seems to be a pet; it never strays far from the grain bowl outside West Whelks. And an owl roosts nearby – wide-eyed and observant – perched on a fishing boat. Actually this one isn't alive but the wood carving makes you take a second glance.

Just past the west quay, I rest on a seat with sea views. But this is no ordinary bench – more railway sleepers have been utilised and it's adorned with a diving helmet sculpture. Whitstable is famous for salvagers who developed an early diving helmet and who brought up booty from ship wrecks including the *Mary Rose*. Behind me is the lifeboat station for these modern day rescuers who've been in the harbour since 1963. The lifeboat's out on its trailer, fortunately just to be admired, though the boat is launched on average twice a week.[8] In front of me, many small boats rest on the west quay waiting to feel salt on their bows when owners have time and inclination. They mourn being grounded, rigging whining in the wind.

Another day, another walk, and I think that I'll check how the harbour is constructed. Memory suggests that the west quay is hollow with supporting wooden poles and the east quay is solid. I head for the harbour mouth, but hear the sound of men's voices and smell fuel just before I see Armac Marine's *Falcon* docked against the east quay completely blocking my view. It dwarfs the boats in the harbour – this metal hulk has men crawling over it, mending and checking. I'll have to wait for another opportunity. When I research to write this chapter I discover that Armac Shipping Services Ltd. was dissolved shortly after I saw the ship at Whitstable. I wonder whether I had the dubious privilege of watching *Falcon* being prepared for scrap. But no, the Internet provides sightings of her in 2012 and 2013 transporting freight to Erith and Goole.[9]

When I finally get to explore the harbour walls, it is low tide, so I can walk near the base of the quay. What I thought were wooden poles are more robust concrete, but nature has taken over – algae, weed and barnacles cover them with a greeny-brown coat. The east quay walls appear to have been painted by a giant artist in brown, green, cream and russet stripes up from the waterline. They suggest years of weathering and growth so I'm surprised to discover that the east quay had new sheet piling in 2006.[10] Huge tractor tyres act as buffers for incoming boats. I smile when I spot a couple of pigeons billing and cooing perched within a tyre.

Nature has a habit of making the most of what surrounds it. Though we do so much to spoil our environment – sometimes accidentally, sometimes deliberately, maybe out of 'necessity' – nature returns, whether it is weeds in pavement cracks, mussels on drainage pipes, vegetation on sea walls or birds in the harbour.

Birds of a Feather…

…flock together. And there they are, beyond the 'No Access' padlocked gate and wrought iron fence, huddled on the harbour wall – a host of birds with dull brown upper-parts and white bellies, twittering *twik-it-it.* They have no problem in flouting the private property laws. The afternoon has already been somewhat mystical, what with discovering the alchemy circle and having been enticed by a stepmother's gleaming red apple left on a nearby groyne. Having resisted its lure, I'd continued my walk to the harbour mouth only to find a hoard of lobster claws draped with blackened seaweed and, in the concrete, my name, NANCY, engraved alongside that of STAN. I'm wondering who Stan might be when the birds grab my attention.

They take flight and, to my surprise, leave their dowdy selves behind. Spread wings display black and white zigzag stripes and their white underbellies glint in the sun and transform to silver shadows; even their call changes, becoming a sharp *tuc-tuc-tuc*. They soar and turn in dazzling synchronisation until with a final swoop they settle again on the harbour wall.

I'm enthralled. I scribble down information in my notebook – colours, patterns, size and calls, and head to the Little Blue Hut to consult my shelf of books. But before I reach the hut I'm entranced again. On one of the 'upturned laundry baskets' sits a gull – bigger than a herring gull – and with a black back. More scribblings.

Back in the hut I flick through the pages of *Coastal Birds* trying to match my mental images and written descriptions with the photos. The flock I'd seen were not right for any kind of gull, more like a wader, but smallish. I look at feather colours, also checking for orangey legs and a dark bill. Turning a page… turnstones. Fortunately, the two photos show the birds in winter plumage; one in their 'at rest' attire and one showing their zigzag wings in flight.

Turnstones are appropriately named because they turn over stones equivalent to their own body weight in their hunt for food. They mainly feed on small invertebrates but will scavenge for scraps and carrion. In summer their plumage is more striking with black and white head markings, a black breast-band and a mottled chestnut brown and black back.[1]

Some turnstones are resident – mainly if they're not breeding – but most are winter visitors. That makes me glad that my residency is at season's turn otherwise I may not have discovered these attractive birds. And again, once I've named them and noted their appearance, I see them along the shingle, in the harbour, even on my walks along the rocks of Ramsgate's coastline. They scurry and peck, sometimes singly but mainly in flocks at this time of year. They are generally unafraid of humans but I have to admit that it's tempting to approach close causing them to flit and flurry and reveal their fascinating patterns and flight formations.

One bird identified; another to find. I'm certain this one is a gull. I look through the different species listed, hoping I won't get caught out by winter feathers as I had with the black-headed gulls. It is a bit of a misnomer calling them summer and winter plumage as the changes occur with breeding and non-breeding seasons and so by the end of September, though we are enjoying a beautiful 'Indian' summer, the birds have put on their 'winter' coats.

Two choices: lesser black-backed gull or great black-backed gull. I wish I'd taken my camera on the walk to have proof, but the image in my mind's eye is fairly clear. I reckon the bird was big enough and the coloration right for a great black-back. The lesser gulls' wings and back are a dark slate grey. The bird I saw was definitely black backed and Big. So, I make my decision and read up about them.

Great black-backed gulls are our largest gull with bulky powerful bodies. They have a black upper body and wings but the wing feathers are white-tipped giving a contrasting trim. Their heads and bellies are white and they have flesh coloured legs and a powerful-looking yellow bill which has a red spot at its tip. Like herring gulls, the young remain as 'ugly ducklings' until their fourth year with scaly black-brown plumage. Great black-backed gulls are opportunistic and will scavenge fish, chicks and eggs from other seabirds, even feed on adult birds and rabbits. They breed in Britain but are less numerous than other species and are mostly seen alone or in their pairs: these facts make me happier that I haven't identified one before. But the book suggests that if you observe a mixed flock of gulls you can usually spot one or two great black-backed among them. How true. As my ability to recognise them grows, I see their blackness among the others' grey.[2]

And one day, away from the Little Blue Hut, I walk around Ramsgate harbour. On the slipway near to where the fishing boats tie up, a small colony of great black-backs are hunkered down. It's hard to tell whether the adolescents are those of the black-backs or herring gulls but I can count over a dozen gulls with striking black backs. No doubt they're waiting for the opportunity to scavenge when the fishing fleet returns. And I'm left wondering if they are new inhabitants or whether they commonly arrive each autumn and I've just been unobservant and ignorant before.

Robin Robertson includes the black-backs amongst his description of the birds at Tynemouth Priory in his poem *Sea Fret:*[3]

> Kittiwakes quarter
> the grey sweep, mewling
> through a squall of sea-wired
> black-backed gulls.

His description resonates in me. I'm becoming entranced by seabirds. And there are more black-backed birds to know – ones that I've spotted before on my walks under the western cliffs along Ramsgate's coast but, sad to say, I'd not really bothered to observe. In my awakening I 'see' them on the shingle outcrop to the east of the Little Blue Hut. This time I want to find out about the flock. Their colours and their calls attract me. They scurry along emitting shrill piping noises as though in constant communication with each other. Their black backs and heads are contrasted by white bellies and startling orange bills, red eyes and pinkish legs. Can you guess?

They are oystercatchers. Like the turnstones, oystercatchers fly as a synchronised flock revealing black and white stripes on their wings and their cry becomes more alarming. But they are larger than turnstones, about the size of the black-headed gulls, but with a different body shape and a long straight bill. They feed on worms and molluscs – more likely mussels and cockles than oysters. During the summer oystercatchers will live inland near gravelly riverbeds or lakes. But these birds tend to move towards the coast as winter approaches and other birds fly in from Norway boosting the numbers of oystercatchers to be seen on the shore. And again, now I know them and can recognise their call, I often find myself absorbed in their scuttle along rocks and shingle, their peck and prod, their flight in co-ordinated arcs with markings displayed.[4]

> Whoever you are, no matter how lonely,
> the world offers itself to your imagination,
> calls to you like the wild geese, harsh and exciting –
> over and over announcing your place
> in the family of things.
>
> from **Wild Geese** by Mary Oliver[5]

It starts slowly – first a line of four; a few days later a skein of ten or more heading into the sunset; next a recognisable 'V'; and, suddenly, seventy, maybe a hundred, flying low over the sea. They come to rest in the shallow water. More winter visitors. I grab my camera and binoculars and rush out of the hut. I know they are geese of some kind – but which kind? They're not very big and in flight they seem to have two contrasting halves – a dark front and a white behind. As I get near to where they are roosting, I approach with caution, uncertain how close I can get before they will take flight. It's not me, but an eager cocker spaniel running through the shallows, that causes lift-off. I snap away with my camera and then continue my walk as they are now resting on water too far off for me to get a clear view.

An hour or so later and I'm heading back. The geese have come onto the shingle and are pecking at the green weed which is in abundance here. This time I'm even more cautious – I take a photo, count off ten steps, another photo, ten steps, another photo, ten steps… I succeed in achieving squelchy shoes and feet, but more satisfactorily I get clear pictures of the geese – roosting, pecking, and when they finally fly, uttering their loud *Krutt, krutt* honk, with wings and neck outstretched towards the sky.

They are Brent Geese, I decide, after scrutinising my photos. They arrive each autumn from breeding grounds in the Arctic and are the smallest of the wild geese in Britain. They have a black head, neck, breast, belly and wings but a white rump giving their two-tone appearance in flight. There is a pale-bellied species but these mainly migrate to Ireland. Adults have a white neck band which I didn't see when watching the birds, but on enlarging some of the photos, it becomes clear.[6]

Again I am glad for my autumnal residency; glad for the chance to learn of new birds; glad to be given the opportunity to stand and stare, to take in and absorb, and allow myself to occupy a different space in "the family of things". And this feast of feathers more than makes up for the absence of goose on Michaelmas Day.

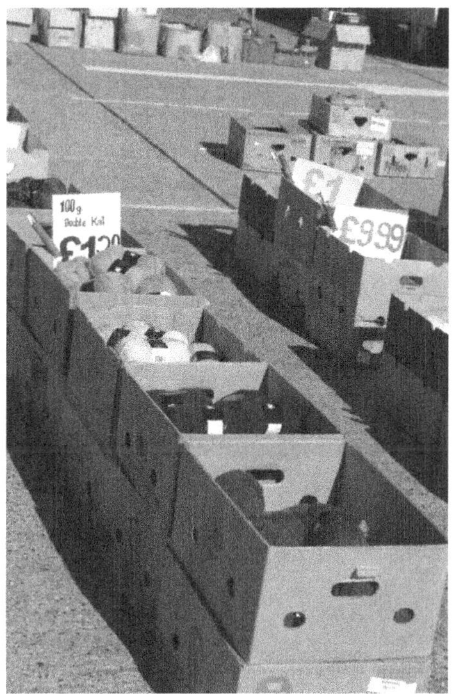

Michaelmas Day

It seems only the more traditional educational establishments, commencing academic years with Michaelmas term, still remember Michaelmas Day. Once upon a time Michaelmas was important as one of the four quarter days of each year: Lady Day, Midsummer, Michaelmas and Christmas. These were when servants were hired, rents were leased and debts should be paid.

Michaelmas Day is the feast of St Michael and All Angels. Michael is one of the top-notch angels, maybe even the chief, and he certainly has his work cut out: according to the all-informative

Wikianswers[1] he is patron saint for forty-eight professions and fifty different places. Among these are bankers and dying people, grocers and haberdashers, paratroopers and mariners. Traditionally his day marked the end of the productive season; the date on which harvesting should be completed. Originally on 10th October, Michaelmas Day was considered the last date blackberries should be eaten, because it marked Lucifer's fall from heaven when he trampled, or spat, on a blackberry bush, poisoning the fruit. Michael, responsible for the eviction, was petitioned to protect people during the approaching dark winter days.

Goose is the food to eat on Michaelmas Day: "Eat a goose on Michaelmas Day, want not for money all the year." A goose would be fattened on the stubble in the fields and killed for the feast. This tradition might have been started by Elizabeth I who was dining on goose when she heard of the Armada's defeat and so proclaimed that everyone should thenceforth eat goose on Michaelmas Day. Alternatively, a goose may have been offered as a 'bribe' if debts couldn't be paid. Michaelmas Day was also called Goose Day and in some places goose fairs or markets would be held.[2]

Michaelmas Day has been celebrated on September 29th since 1752 when the calendar was rejigged.[3] And September 29th in 2011 falls on a Thursday – market day for Whitstable. So I decide to investigate. I arrive at the Little Blue Hut shortly after nine on a morning of glorious sunshine and a low tide about to turn. I have never seen the sea such a rich colour or so calm – my immediate thoughts are of emulsion in a painting tray ready to be put on the walls of a baby boy's nursery. A solitary canoeist contrasts the water with his yellow boat. The turbines are white and gleaming in the sun but behind them the horizon holds a rose and mauve haze. As the tide flows in, the water over the spit is bright ultramarine. It's on this day that I notice the spit fisherman whose golden hair and T-shirt are as vivid as the surrounding colours. There's also a cormorant on its outpost and the Thames Barge is heading out of harbour, sails furled, but still a magnificent sight. Around my hut, crane flies are dancing. This is surely going to be a good day.

I set off towards the town. I keep to the seafront for a while; amused by a line of gulls perched on consecutive groyne posts in parallel with a line of buoys bobbing on the water. I walk past the Hotel Continental and along the road to the main car park where the market is held. A set of green and white gazebos have been erected in one corner. There's a mixture of stalls: fruit and veg, eggs, bread, packaged food, household goods, socks and shoes, and a stall with thick padded jackets which normally would have expected brisk trade by the end of September. In fact, no-one's doing a brisk trade – there are only a few customers and most, like me, seem to be browsers rather than purchasers.

My eye is attracted away from the stalls by row upon row of boxes of brightly coloured knitting wool. I have a secret passion for wool and material. I knit and sew but I also just enjoy revelling in an array of colour and texture. These boxes lead me to another part of the market – where goods are either on trestle tables or laid out on the ground. These stallholders must be glad of the fine weather. Here is a more eclectic array: worn but exotic carpets, second-hand brass handles and locks, guitars and wind instruments, LPs and '78s' with a wind-up record player, vibrant paintings, vintage clothes, genie lamps and a junk stall with a faded multi-coloured parasol. Amongst this hotchpotch a police-van is parked and two officers keep an eye on the proceedings from behind their dark shades.

But there are no geese for sale. Nor even a Michaelmas Daisy, named for their late flowering between August and early October:[4]

The Michaelmas Daisies, among dede weeds,
Bloom for St Michael's valorous deeds.
And seem the last of flowers that stood
Till the feast of St Simon and St Jude.

I suppose the market is fairly typical, similar to the one that appears on the town centre streets of Ramsgate. But I remember from my childhood the Friday market in Kettering as full of delights, and crowded with people. Kettering was called a market town. And on the rare occasions when I went with my mother on the train to Leicester market – well, that kept my senses satisfied for weeks. This market holds some interest, and like pedlars and traders travelling the country in medieval times, it has a provisional feel. I guess it's the lack of bustle that disappoints.

I decide to walk back through the harbour. I immediately sense a contrasting animation. The cockle pyramid is a frenzy of feeding, squabbling, squawking gulls and others fight over a dropped hunk of bread. People rush or amble, purposeful or relaxed but enlivened by their environment. As I walk past the buildings at Bretts a smile floods my face: a whole flock of black-headed gulls is perched in the troughs of the corrugated iron roof using them as ready-made camp-beds.

I tread the beach path; a lady cycles past on an old-fashioned sit-up-and-beg bicycle with her purchases protruding from a basket on her handlebars. Her golden hair flows down to her waist and she has a matching yellow belt tied loosely round a black shift dress. And another character grabs my attention – a man stands at the water's edge throwing bread into the sea, wearing a bright green coat and purple jogging bottoms. He has a tanned, chiselled face and tousled hair and the phrase pops into my head: "Cast your bread upon the waters,/ for after many days you will find it again." [5] What is he hoping for? All my market disappointment is shed by the time I see the cormorant again, perched and preening with its wings outstretched.

The sea, by now, is almost at high tide and a lovely turquoise colour. The haze has vanished leaving a clear horizon and Essex in view. Despite it being Thursday, a work day, many people are making the most of the sunshine – stripped off and sunbathing, even swimming in the sea. A man paddles his kayak parallel to the shore, yellow blades dipping in and out of the water.

I sit on the grass outside my hut, write up my notes and begin to let a poem germinate in my mind. I'm so impressed with the sea's colours today that I start to dream of a woman who is clothed by the sea. As the tide turns and begins to recede, the spit fisherman reappears. I stay on for sunset and I'm treated to a glorious golden ball haloed with yellow, tangerine and red which, as it sinks, turns the horizon into a flaming red and indigo sheen and the sea into a pastel pink and blue balm worthy of the greatest Impressionist artist. People walking the spit appear as dark silhouettes. Unable to paint, I take photos in an attempt to capture something of the beauty. It is one of those evenings when I'm awed by nature's colours.

And the show doesn't stop. The sky darkens; stars and Jupiter glow. Only the moon doesn't make an appearance. It's a couple of days past new moon; the high tides are high and the low tides are low, but the moon's still hidden from view.

Seaside Special

Sunshine, Saturday, down on the beach in the evening sun,
Sunshine, Saturday, down on the beach we're going to have some fun,
Now is the time to be dancing, the music has just begun…

It's easy to lose time surfing the Internet. As I start to draft this chapter, lyrics slip unbidden into my mind. A blast from the past. Though I've not thought about the song in years, once the tune's stuck in my head, it becomes imperative to find out more. I think it's the theme song for *Seaside Special* – a BBC Saturday night summer variety show. Wikipedia tells me the show ran between 1975 and 1979, broadcast from a big top located at varying seaside resorts.[1] I discover a glancing mention of the song stuck in my head, but all the You-tube clips give Mike Batt's *Summertime Special* as the signature tune. I find clips of comedy by Ken Dodd, hosting by Tony Blackburn, and singing by Lulu and Abba.[2] But not my song… I suppose it could belong to the less successful 1980s revival. I resume my search…but after a 'wasted' hour, I decide this is a memory that will have to remain uncorroborated.

Memory can be fickle. I had contemplated this as I was staring at a sunset. I'd wondered if I would recall it accurately so took photographs hoping they would act as an aide-memoire. But now another worry surfaces – are the colours in the photos a true reflection of the colours that I saw? I just have to hope that my camera, laptop and printer are of suitable sophistication to reproduce images realistically.

On my very first evening as writer-in-residence I stayed to watch the sunset. The photos show a sparkling creamy-gold disc sinking towards the western horizon, with yellow-gold rays tinting nearby cloud edges. The surrounding sky and cloud mass are mauve and pink. As the sun sinks, small clouds in front of it give quirky sunglasses and nose features. Approaching the horizon, the sun bulges, flattens and becomes more yellow. The rays disappear as it sinks into a blue-purple haze, less and less of the disc is visible until finally, it sets. Meanwhile in the east a pale-pink full moon has risen in a blue-grey sky. As the sky darkens the moon appears whiter and then golden, and dark splodges are splashed across its surface. The sky deepens from a blur of pastelly shades until it is navy blue and the moon is high.

So there's my primary school description of the sunset. Not very poetic and probably not all that accurate in terms of colour names. But it gives the gist of what I saw. I know colours can vary at sunset but I wonder if they are usually similar. The flattening, bulging disc also intrigues. Two days later I watch again… This time there's no corresponding moon rise as it's now rising later in the evening. The sunset colours are more vivid. The sun appears a luminescent deep yellow with a surrounding halo and the sky near the sun is tinged golden and orange, while the upper sky is a deep cornflower blue. As the sun sinks lower and behind cloud its luminescence spreads to a golden blur; the sky nearby is buttercup-yellow and deep orange. The sun emerges below the clouds as a squashed yellow disc, the sky turns flamingo and orange with some buttery streaks and, as the sun sets, takes on red as well, and the nearby clouds are purplish-mauve.

Still not a very poetic description but hopefully it shows the similarities and differences between the two. I decide it's time to research sunset and colour…

I return to the book, *Color and Light in Nature.*[3] This was a bit of a lucky find – a punt among the second-hand books available on Amazon. Printed in 1995, its jacket is somewhat faded but the pages are full of words and formulae, diagrams and photographs. I'm glad of my science background so I can understand those aspects of the book but there's plenty of descriptive information. The section about the colour and brightness of the low sun begins:

> As the sun approaches the horizon, its colour changes from dazzling white to bright yellow, orange and even to deep red. No two setting (or rising) suns are alike, yet they all have one thing in common: they are dimmer and redder than when they are overhead.

The colour changes are mainly to do with light scattering. When the sun is overhead not much light is removed from a sunbeam due to the optical depth of the sky being relatively small. Nearer the horizon, however, light passes through many more air molecules which scatter it. Shorter wavelengths are scattered more frequently than longer ones. Also, water vapour and ozone absorb short wavelengths. From our viewpoint, it appears that blues and purples are missing and so we see the sun as yellow, orange or red.

Particles of dust and smoke also affect the sun's colour as they are efficient scatterers. These cause the sun to appear redder, so there can be particularly spectacular sunsets when the air is particle-laden such as after the volcanic eruption of Eyjafjallajökull, Iceland, in 2010. Also near the sea, water droplets in the atmosphere increase scattering. I suppose, when I watched the sunset on the second occasion, there must have been more particles or water vapour in the sky producing a more vivid sunset.

The halo surrounding the sun is called an aureole. It's always present but during the day appears white and is difficult to gaze at because of the sun's brightness. As the sun turns to yellow, the aureole is more easily seen. Scattering from different particles is again the cause of this phenomenon.[4]

But scattering and particles can't be blamed for the squashed appearance of the sun as it heads towards the horizon. This is a different physics effect – refraction. Do you remember playing with prisms in a science lab and seeing how a ray of light changes direction or how a stick in a glass of water appears to bend? These effects are due to light being refracted. And so is the flattened sun. The sun is not a pinpoint – it has breadth. As it approaches the horizon light from the bottom of the disc passes through more air and is therefore refracted to a greater extent than light coming from the top of the disc. This causes the bottom of the sun to seem pushed up. The amount of flattening depends on temperature and the particles in the air, and our observation point – standing on a mountain the sun will appear to flatten more than when we are at sea level.[5]

It is satisfying to find out the explanations for some of the things I've seen. So much goes on colour-wise around sunset. Even when the sun is below the horizon it continues to illuminate the sky – this is the time we call twilight or dusk and different effects are seen in the west and in the east.

As the sun sinks below the horizon the west sky becomes the yellowish colour of the twilight arch which grows as the zenith sky darkens. The arch is caused by sunlight scattered in the atmosphere which is still seen even though the sun is below the horizon. Meanwhile in the east the bluish earth-shadow is capped by a pinkish anti-twilight arch. Next, the western sky continues to have a bright twilight arch which is yellow or orange but shows purple too; easterly the earth shadow and anti-twilight arch begin to fade and the sky becomes a more diffuse blue. By the time the sun is 6° below the horizon the earth shadow has vanished and the twilight arch has become orangey-red. The eastern sky continues to darken, the western has a red afterglow which eventually darkens too and the sky takes on its night-time appearance.

Twilight is divided into stages, dependent upon the sun's position. From sunset to the sun being 6° below the horizon is civil twilight; -6° to -12° is nautical twilight, and -12° to -18° is astronomical twilight. By the time the sun is that low the sky is dark and stars can be seen.[6]

Armed with my newfound knowledge I decide to stay for another sunset. It's the glorious Michaelmas Day. The evening sky is clear and I'm treated to an almost 'textbook' sunset. I can see the earth shadow and a pink anti-twilight arch which creates a pastel blue and pink sea. In the west the yellow aureole becomes a yellow twilight arch which then takes on orange and red hues and the surrounding sky has a purple tinge. It's so rewarding to see something you have read about happening in real time. And addictive. A few days later I decide to stay again. Disappointment! The sun fails to break through the cloud cover – the earth shadow can't be seen and there's very little in the way of colour change in the western sky.

Still, I can't feel too downhearted. I now understand something of sunset. But what of the colours? I noticed that in *Color and Light in Nature* the descriptions still use basic blue, pink, red, yellow, orange and purple without trying to describe different shades and hues. I turn to an artist colour book. This gives me lots of different shades for each colour – bright circles in rows along the page but the names are based upon the paints from which they can be mixed. So in yellows there are 60 dots but the names run something like – Naples yellow 1, Naples yellow light, Naples yellow deep, Naples yellow extra. Still, there are lemons, primary, primrose, cadmium, brilliant, aureolin and Indian yellows.[7]

Another chart gives me a more descriptive set of words. Winifred Nicholson in 1944 created a Colour and Substance Chart with 105 different colour words.[8] This provides some interesting names: azure, emerald, larkspur, mustard, damson and cabbage. I wonder if paint charts for budding room designers would help so I search online for Dulux colour schemes.[9] In their overview of yellow the colours selected seem pinkish more than yellow – pale citrus, wild primrose, lunar falls, daffodil white, buttermilk and ivory lace. The names are more imaginative though and, delving further into the site, I discover a panoply of yellow colour names: buttercup fool, golden fern, banana dream, lemon chiffon… It's amazing how often things of nature turn up in the names. A final look for colour names and I find charts on Wikipedia – an amazing alphabetical list of colours – amber, arylide yellow, chartreuse, citrine…[10]

So now I'm better equipped with names, slightly further forward in my musings, but I'm left wondering how many colour names actually have meaning to somebody without the relevant colour on view. Would you really have any idea what 'lunar falls' is like? So often we use yellow-coloured things to describe yellow colours – banana, lemon or buttercup. That feels a bit like a circular argument. And there's still my original problem – colours on a chart or in a paint tin are discrete whereas in nature colours intermingle and swirl.

In reading about sunset, I also discover about sunrise – dawn is the twilight of the rising sun and the colour changes are similar to sunset but in the reverse order and on the opposite side of the sky. It is not 'darkest just before dawn'. It may well be coldest as the earth and atmosphere have been cooling through the night but light and dark are more symmetrically arranged around midnight (Greenwich Mean Time). Two factors may make sunrise appear different to sunset: our eyes are no longer daylight adapted and therefore see colour changes more clearly, and generally the air is less full of pollutants and particles in the morning, particularly in urban areas.[11]

There's only one way to find out more. I set my alarm for 6am and leave home as the sky's beginning to lighten. Driving along I worry I'll have missed all the colour changes by the time I reach the hut. At 7am I'm stood on the slope waiting for official sunrise of 7.26am. The eastern sky is a rich flamingo orange and the zenith sky is slate blue. The sky lightens, taking on rose and mauve hues and as they fade, a yellowish tinge heralds the sun's rise. The sky becomes golden yellow as the sun climbs higher. Today the sun rises through clouds. They become lined with gold. I've never seen this when watching sunsets. Again I search for an explanation: the edge of a cloud is less thick than its centre so when it's back lit, the light pierces through the edge and shows itself as a 'silver lining' or, with the rising sun, a golden one.

In summer the sun rises and sets over the sea at Tankerton. But by autumn I have to wait for the sun to emerge from behind the buildings on Marine Parade. With the change from summer into autumn and then winter, sunrise and sunset head further south and the sun rises three minutes later and sets about three minutes earlier each day. So our days shorten. We must wait for winter solstice for the reverse process to begin.

Season's Turn

To every thing there is a season, and a time to every purpose under heaven.
Ecclesiastes 3:1[1]

Autumn equinox and it's another lovely sunny day at the Little Blue Hut. I arrive and sit outside, no coat, just a cardigan. There's a blue sky, and on the corresponding blue sea, a speed boat pulls a water-skier. Whoops! Down he goes, splash, into the boat's backwash. Water-skiing looks graceful and fun… until the fall. I remember the unicyclist I'd seen the previous evening – no tumble for him. He cycled all the way up the slope, precariously balanced on his one wheel, but looking full of confidence, grin spread across his face.

My thoughts turn to my daughter who phoned with the surprising news that she's going to run the Brighton Marathon… which brings me to consider equality: men have run the marathon in the modern Olympics since 1908, women only since 1984.[2] So many things women have been 'allowed' to do in the last century: vote, fight in the forces, be Prime Minister, pole vault… But are we equal? Can it happen and what does equality mean?

I reflect how my life has altered in the last few years – from full-on mothering of five children to being able to reside for six weeks in a beach hut. With only one child left at home, and he in his last year at school, Mum is no longer in so much demand. I've begun finding a new place of equilibrium for myself – one in which my needs and aspirations play a bigger role. I smile, enjoying that thought. I contemplate an idea for a poem about the slope's crows and watch the water-skier take flight again.

"A time for every purpose." This biblical phrase is possibly better known from, *Turn! Turn! Turn!,* the Pete Seeger song made famous by *The Byrds* in 1965.[3] I was a toddler then, so don't remember the original, but it's one of those songs which has entered the popular music repertoire from folk clubs to school assemblies. A season for everything. Well, it's a long time since I participated in a school assembly but there is still much I can and want to learn.

Equinox is about equality, being in equilibrium. It happens twice a year – March and September – when the tilt of the Earth's axis lines up with the sun. This means that the subsolar point (the place on the Earth's surface where the centre of the sun is directly overhead) is at the equator. In Britain we count these days as the start of a changing season – spring and autumn. Summer begins when the subsolar point is at its furthest north, over the Tropic of Cancer, and winter when the subsolar point is over the Tropic of Capricorn – the summer and winter solstices. If the earth wasn't at a tilt we wouldn't have the same seasonal changes.[4]

I learnt, as a child, that seasons shift on the 21st of their respective months – March, June, September and December. But in 2011 the autumn equinox falls on 23rd September. It seems that the dates aren't fixed in stone. The earth has an elliptical orbit around the sun. In January the earth is closest to the sun and moving at its fastest speed around it. So we tend to arrive at spring equinox a day early. The converse is true for autumn equinox – we get there late by a day or so. Leap years, intended to get us back into 'right timing' with our circuit around the sun, also play a part. The result – there can be a couple of days variation in the date of the equinox.

Equinox comes from two Latin words – *aequus* (equal) and *nox* (night). The name was coined to suggest that day and night are of equal duration with sunrise and sunset six hours either side of midday. But as in life, some are more equal than others. I look at Whitstable sunrise and sunset charts: sunrise is at 0643 and sunset is at 1853. We're still on British Summer Time. This accounts for the times being around seven am and pm as we are running an hour ahead of the sun.

But day is longer than night. They're not equal. This, I discover, is due to a number of factors. The sun is a disc, not just a pinpoint. We count sunrise and set at the moment when the top of the sun appears or disappears over the horizon whereas the equinox point is based on the position of the centre of the sun. Also the sun's light is refracted by the atmosphere which means it appears to rise before and set after it actually does.

These two effects lengthen daytime by about 14 minutes at the equator and, because the earth spins at an angle, by more towards the poles. However, local sunrise is also affected by landscape. When land, buildings or trees block the view, sunrise will be later and sunset earlier. This counterbalances some of the other gains.

For Whitstable, in 2011, the dates which are more equally balanced between day and night are 25th and 26th September.

Another thing puzzles. These dates are when the sun is over the equator and the tropics, but they mark the start of a season. Surely they should be the centre point of each season?

We have seasons' lag. The earth in the northern hemisphere continues to warm up after we have had the northernmost sunrise at the summer solstice, so the warmest days generally happen in July and August. Though summer solstice is sometimes called Midsummer's Day, that's not actually true. Likewise, the earth takes time to rewarm after the winter solstice and so the coldest days are in January and February. The reverse is true for the southern hemisphere.[5]

This autumn equinox, I chat to a man from Canterbury. He likes to swim in the sea and tells me this is the latest date in any year that he's swum in England. He proclaims it a moral cleansing. I feel restless, with my thoughts flitting, but I don't fancy joining him for a swim. Instead I decide to walk and explore more of Whitstable.

I set off along the promenade, through the harbour and end up in the town at Horsebridge. The *Horsebridge Arts and Community Centre* is a favourite haunt. I'm one half of a poetic duo but I live in Ramsgate and my partner-in-poetry in Maidstone; Whitstable is one of our midway meeting points. Often on Sundays we hire a workshop space. The friendly staff are always happy to help. The centre was opened in 2004 as part of a redevelopment to provide housing and social facilities. But the Horsebridge area has a long history, taking its name from the jetty used by the horses when they carried the catch from the fishing boats.[6]

I continue my walk. Whitstable has an eclectic mix of shops, with only a sprinkling of the usual high street names. There are

Boots, Budgens, Holland & Barrett, Costa but these are a minority among emporiums of wooden toys, kites, clothes, retro furniture, fish shops, art galleries, cheese, lavender, wine and oysters… It is one of the few places that have managed to resist the pull of mediocrity – even the handful of charity shops set out their wares with style.

The shops are one delight; the alleys another. Whitstable grew up around the main road from Canterbury but alleyways developed as residents wanted good access to the sea. They proved useful, particularly for smugglers needing quick and hidden routes. My favourite is Squeeze Gut Alley, apparently once known as Granny Bell's Alley because a grandmother of sixteen children lived there. Its present name is apt. At one end, the walls on each side loom high and dark and the alley bottle-necks. You literally have to squeeze your gut, or at least turn sideways, to pass through and out onto Island Wall.[7]

I spend some time exploring alleys and then take a road I've never been down before. I walk parallel with the railway and find myself at the golf course. This must be the one that was flooded in 1953. I can see why; its greens are below sea level. I head along a footpath through the middle of the course which I suspect will lead me to the seafront at the western end of Whitstable. There's a dearth of golfers – perhaps they are early morning devotees before they commute to London. Whitstable has become a favourite location for those moving out of the city for a 'better' life whether permanently or just for a weekend break.

But the lack of golfers means others are enjoying the grass. Gulls and crows waddle and peck and, in a marshy patch between my path and the greens, I spot a bird I've not seen before. Its body shape, long legs and bill suggest that it's some kind of wader. But which kind? I head back to the hut to try to discover its name.

Migration, Murmuration and Mystery

Admiration is insufficient. Careful observation is needed, especially for a novice like me. Caught up in the excitement of the moment, I didn't pay enough attention to the bird's characteristics – didn't make notes or take photos. I'm reliant on my mental image.

I flick through the pages of the *Larousse Pocket Guide* to find the waders.[1] The bird I saw had yellow-brownish plumage. I'm careful to consider winter coats. It's difficult to decide: water rail, corn crake, plover, sandpiper, dunlin and stint are all too small; the stone curlew is a better size but only a summer visitor and has a short bill. Possibly it was a juvenile ruff, a bar-tailed godwit in winter coat, an Eurasian curlew, a snipe or maybe a redshank, though I don't recall a red bill and legs. I pick up another book; see if it helps. The illustrations vary somewhat: the snipe appears to have longer legs. This makes me teeter towards my bird being one. But I think I remember a curved bill and a fairly large body…

I plump for the curlew. *Larousse* tells me they winter in the south of England, liking estuaries, marshes and adjacent fields. So that fits. But they're generally gregarious, forming large flocks and my bird was solitary. It's the buff and brown colouring and the long bill that steer my choice to curlew. But I will never be totally sure for though I've walked that route several times, I've never spotted a similar bird on the golf course, or anywhere else.

Another day, a different mystery – a 'singing tree' – a conifer full of chorusing birds. I stop and stare. What kind of birds provide this glorious performance? Perhaps they're from a fairy tale in which a good witch enchanted the tree, transformed the fir cones into songbirds. They sing to bring a handsome prince who will rescue the spellbound princess.

In reality, they're more ordinary. I notice similar birds on roofs, chimney pots and television aerials. One day, they are massed on the masts of the small boats on the slipway and some bathe in pools of rainwater collected on the boat covers. Close-up I recognise them: starlings.

Starlings are common birds in Britain, known for their swaggering strut, the green and purple iridescence on their black wings and their white-spotted breasts in winter. The young are dowdy with grey coats; born helpless and fluffy. The following spring, as I wait to pick up a friend, I spot a starling family pecking in the station car park. I can identify father, mother and a single offspring.

They call with a piercing *schrien* or hard *spett-spett* but their singing is composed of whistles, chatters and clicks, and mimicry of other birds and noises. So it's not always easy to recognise starlings by their song. But in winter, they characteristically flock together and especially mesmerising is a starling murmuration.

...they are acrobats
in the freezing wind.
And now in the theatre of air
they swing over buildings,
dipping and rising;
they float like one stippled star
that opens,
becomes for a moment fragmented,

then closes again;

from **Starlings in Winter** by Mary Oliver [2]

The aerial dance usually takes place at dusk as they settle for the night. Starlings spend the day in small groups feeding, or perched in treetops and on roofs. They roost in much larger numbers in woodlands, reed beds, cliffs and buildings, for protection, warmth and to communicate about good feeding sites. As they gather to roost the murmuration begins – a wheeling, twisting plume of smoke created as thousands of starlings fly in synchrony. I was lucky to see a small murmuration one day when driving home from the beach hut. The starlings circled and danced over the fields inland from the coast. Unfortunately, I couldn't stop to see where they finally landed.

They fly in intricate shapes without crashing into each other by copying their neighbours. Each individual starling concentrates on the six or so birds that surround it and mimics their movements. As a result any tiny deviation by one bird is magnified by the whole flock creating the rippling, swirling patterns. They fly together for protection from predators such as peregrine falcons and sparrowhawks. The murmuration responds faster in the presence of a predator. As one bird shifts to fly away from an attacker, those around react, which causes the next birds to alter their flight, and then the next, and so the twisting wave propagates through the whole flock.[3]

Numbers of starlings are swollen each winter as birds fly in from Eastern Europe. They certainly seem plentiful in Tankerton and Whitstable. But the RSPB has designated starlings with red status because of declining numbers in England and elsewhere.[4] At one time murmurations were a common sight over most cities – in 1949 so many starlings roosted on Big Ben that they stopped the clock. It seems Rome is the city of the moment with an influx of several million birds each winter. The swarms are spectacular but worrying. Starling droppings are acidic and could cause considerable damage to Rome's ancient monuments, besides annoying living residents whose car paint may need re-spraying.[5]

I'm also party to another bird 'dance'. One day, after using the public toilets I take a short-cut back to the hut across the slope. Suddenly I'm surrounded by a flock of birds flying a few feet above my head seemingly oblivious to, or uncaring of, my presence. Their white bodies and dark wings make me think they must be swallows and I assume they are feeding on the wing before they migrate south for the winter. They are silent and I'm entranced as I watch them. It is one of those good-to-be-alive moments.

Weeks later I explore further up the coast. Between Herne Bay and Reculver lie Beltinge and Bishopstone. Their beaches are undeveloped and have a backdrop of soft rock cliffs. In these cliffs, near Bishopstone, are hundreds of holes. The penny drops. But I have to wait until the following summer to prove my hunch – I had seen sand martins. These are the smallest of the swallow-like birds with a shallow forked tail. Their underparts are white and they have sandy brown wings and characteristic breast bands.

Sand martins, like swallows, are summer visitors. They are gregarious, existing in flocks that swoop and feed together. That summer I walk through the meadow on the cliff-top above the holes and there are two, five, ten, twenty, more, sand martins darting and feeding. I head down the path onto the beach – each of the holes is occupied. Using binoculars, I can see parents swooping in to feed the young that perch and squeak, beaks open to receive.

Tankerton Slopes are better known for rock pipits. Or so I thought. The RSPB website map[6] doesn't identify the North Kent coast as a place for pipits and the signs that were up at Tankerton with information about the rock pipits have disappeared. But pipits are here – I can see them. These smallish birds have upperparts streaked grey-brown with off-white underparts, and breast and flanks also heavily streaked. They are well camouflaged on the shingle beach. Perhaps they are just winter visitors to this coast but I can definitely hear their sharp *pseet* calls. They gather in the bushes and sing, but if I try to get close to photograph, they first go silent and then flit away with darting flight.

> When they sing from the harbour wall, amongst
> the soured lines and ten-fathom creels,
> it sounds like an apprenticeship for something more
> auspicious…
>
> from **Rock Pipits** by John Burnside [7]

The couple of wood pigeons waddling the slope by my hut are much easier to photograph. *Columba Palumbus* are the biggest of the pigeons and have wonderful colouring with their pinkish breast;

green, white and purple patch on neck; grey and black wings and tail; and white neck-flash and bar on open wings. They peck and coo and take flight with a clatter. They seem like fat country gentlemen in comparison to the more furtive 'town' cousins.

Feral pigeons are some of the commonest birds in our towns. They are descended from escaped domestic doves and racing pigeons and their plumage can be a riotous mix according to their individual heritage. I think of being pigeon-holed, pigeon-toed or pigeon-hearted and wonder how such phrases became part of our language.

I'm not too keen on pigeon-holing, but pigeons are generally considered a nuisance as they will nest on any spare ledge or in deserted buildings. Their droppings are not only messy but, like starlngs, can cause damage due to their acidity. Along the seafront at Whitstable are a number of wooden cottages. Most are attractive dwellings for residents or used as holiday homes. But at Stag Cottage, pigeons stare from the windows. On the road, the cottage looks like a normally occupied house, but from the beach... Is it a magical place? Does the good witch live here, or her malevolent cousin?

Unfortunately, the story behind the pigeons of Stag Cottage is no fairy tale.[8] In a dispute between the owner and Whitstable Oyster Company the house has been divided in two by a stud wall. The Oyster Company claim that part of Stag Cottage is on their land and consequently belongs to them. The argument seems to hinge around the high water line and how that may have changed over the years. The owner is left with half a bathroom and his life disrupted in a dispute that's been ongoing for nearly a decade. Meanwhile the pigeons have made the most of the situation and taken occupancy of the Oyster Company's part. One white pigeon sits in the uppermost window as a queen surveying her kingdom. It's pleasanter to imagine a fairy tale plot than be faced with the seeming pettiness of reality.

Initiation Rites

Ring-a-ring o' roses…
Spinning and spinning and spinning around…
They marched them up to the top of the hill…
Jack fell down and broke his crown… [1]

I've seen groups before, gathered or walking past: extended families enjoying the unexpected sunshine; Japanese boys caught in a downpour, not a coat among them; European teenagers laughing, chatting and photographing; more teenagers, English this time, on the shingle, geography fieldwork in mind, tape measures and metre rules in hand; a coach party of grannies headed for the market; a walking bus of children, fluorescent coated, indulging in chalk pictures on the promenade. This group is different. They arrive as the sun nears the horizon. It had been an overcast day but as dusk approached, the clouds cleared a little to reveal a cornflower blue sky, the remaining clouds tinged with damask rose. I'd decided to stay for the sunset. But here is promise of a different spectacle.

I'm not good at estimating but there must be at least fifty parading down the slope, 'uniformed' in trousers, shirts and matching ties. Though a few lark about, there's a sense of purpose in their manner. Once on the shingle they adopt poses of legs astride and hands in pockets or folded across chests, clustered in twos and threes – lads emerging from adolescence into manhood, overseen by one silver-haired chief. Eight are thrust from the ranks. Stripped off to reveal lily-white chests, they're encouraged into the water. They stand and shiver, begin to play-fight, before joining together in a circle to enact a good semblance of Ring-a-ring of roses. Only when all have been fully immersed several times are they allowed back onto the beach.

Lined up on the shingle, each is handed a two litre bottle which I suspect contains something more than its apparent innocuous lemonade. Drink and spin is the next routine, round and round, faster and faster, until all the liquid is drunk and the lads are sick. Each is watched over by a mentor who once this trick's accomplished, sends his dizzy mentee towards the slope.

Three wait on guard, one a third of the way up, one two-thirds, one at the top. Barefoot the initiates run to the first guard and are sent back down, up to the second and down again, stagger to the top and then they are forced onto the ground to roll the whole incline of the slope. Those who can stand at the bottom receive a rugby shirt, handshakes and hugs of acceptance. For one, it is all too much. He finishes his rolling by an overflowing bin. And there he remains, green-faced, stomach-retching, creating his own poignant metaphor, until someone eventually takes pity on him, gives him a top to wear and vaguely watches over him until he can stand again.

I'm not the only spectator. Others have come out of their beach huts or stopped on their evening promenade, including a dog, so large and thick-coated it looks as if it shares genes with a brown bear. Its presence adds to the somewhat surreal situation. It is one of those occasions which, from the outside, seem somewhat nonsensical. You wonder: Why? What makes this necessary? Or fun? Will they all continue to view it as normal behaviour later in life.

The things we do to be accepted. Will the one who 'failed' ever know acceptance within the pack? Possibly his eventual prowess on the rugby field will be sufficient or perhaps, because of this failure, he may never get the chance to prove himself. As they stand around, soaked in sea water and testosterone, I decide to go for a walk. The sun is trying to break through the re-gathering clouds, so I head west hoping to catch a sunset from on the spit. In fact, the sun never re-emerges and the grey clouds have only a faint pink tinge. But I am treated to a geese fly-past – one of the first of the season.

By the time I return to the hut, the lads are gone. To their credit, there's no trace of their former presence – no litter left on the beach, not even the originally discarded plastic bottles. Not all are so tidy-minded. One day I find firework shells stuck in the shingle, their cardboard box strewn alongside. I photograph, wonder what celebration they'd marked, then pick them up to put in a bin. Another day an empty cigarette packet lies on the steps of a nearby beach hut. As the blue of the packet exactly matches the hut's paint, it seems a deliberate placement. I see Swan Vestas spilled out like a deserted pick-a-stick game and a shredded, lurid purple tennis ball, besides discarded litter and strandline debris.

But it's not just modern people who leave things behind. In Whitstable museum are Roman Red Samian Ware pots. Fishermen have been catching these in their nets for centuries; many still intact and in good enough condition to be used by local people for making puddings. The pots probably came from shipwrecks or cargo jettisoned in a storm.[2] Even older, the fossils found in the London Clay bring 'treasure' seekers to this part of the coast.

And some people deliberately set out to make a difference to their surroundings. Tankerton has its own castle. Actually, it's currently claimed by Whitstable and after a spell as the Council Offices is now run by the Whitstable Castle Trust to provide "a unique and special venue for weddings, private parties, local classes, corporate and community events".[3]

But it was first known as Tankerton Tower. It's not an ancient monument and, like the cannons perched on the slope nearby, is decorative rather than providing real protection from marauders. Only the beacon basket, close to the cannons, is a true reminder of historic invaders (and that is a replica). Set up from coast to city the beacons were lit to warn of imminent attack in an era long before telegraphs, telephones and digital media. The successive lighting of beacons relayed a message far quicker than horseback riders.

Tankerton Tower was originally built by Charles Pearson in 1790. His wife had inherited the Manor of Tankerton and associated copperas works. By this time copperas was in decline, so Pearson demolished the works and used some of the bricks to build the tower. The Pearsons mainly lived in Greenwich but came to Tankerton each summer. As Pearson's family increased he needed larger accommodation and so by 1821, an extension had been added. Pearson shifted his local interest from copperas to the railway, being one of the original investors in the Crab and Winkle Line. Unfortunately he died in 1828, two years before the railway was opened. The Tower was inherited by his son, who sold it to his cousin, Wynn Ellis.

Mr Ellis had made a fortune from the silk business and he was Liberal MP for Hertford. He was married to Mary Maria Pearson, a great niece of Charles, who lived with him in Hatfield or London. Ellis bought Tankerton Tower in 1836 for his mistress, Susan Lloyd, and her two children, Arthur and Susan Alinda. Ellis repaired the original building and created a new west wing and bell tower. He added North and South Lodges and another lodge house near the main gateway. The whole estate contained fields, cottages, gravel pits, stables, summerhouses, an ice house, gardens and, of course, the beach.

After his death in 1875, Susan Alinda became Lady of the Manor. She died in 1884 and the property passed to her brother who had become the Reverend Arthur Graystone. He died two years later and the estate was inherited by his elder son, Sydney Wynn Graystone who moved to Devon in 1890 and sold Tankerton Tower to a solicitor, Mr E. Newton Robinson.

Robinson was a businessman. The Bank Holiday Act of 1871 encouraged people to have time off, take a holiday. Robinson thought the Tankerton estate would make a great seaside resort. He built a road through the grounds and sold off building plots. However, his venture ran into financial difficulties and the Tower and land were mortgaged and subsequently rented out. In 1897 they were bought by Thomas Adams who added a billiard room with servants' quarters above. Following Adams' death in 1902, his widow remained at the Tower until 1920 when it became the property of Albert Mallandain, a paper manufacturer, who used it as a summer residence. He made interior changes including adding a new staircase and extensive additional oak panelling to match the original design.

When the Mallandains retired to Surrey in 1935, Whitstable Urban District Council bought the property and it became the Council offices. Concerts and dances were held on the site of the tennis courts, the bowling green was created in 1936 and the gardens opened to the public in 1948. With local government re-organisation in 1972 the building became vacant until, at the instigation of The Whitstable Society, the Castle Centre Association took over its management in 1975.[4]

And thus Tankerton Tower changed into Whitstable Castle. The whole area now comes under the auspices of Canterbury City Council, but Tankerton still likes to consider itself as separate from its neighbours, Whitstable to the west and Swalecliffe to the east.

The Circus is in Town

When walking the streets or promenade, it's difficult to establish where Whitstable ends and Tankerton starts or where Tankerton ends and Swalecliffe begins. Or vice versa. There seem to be no cut-off points, no no-man's land between places, not even a sign announcing the start of one, the end of another. I decide to consult the A-Z Street Atlas.[1] Again, no boundary markers, only names across the areas they approximately cover. My guess is that the boundary between Tankerton and Swalecliffe runs along Herne Bay Road which itself runs from the coast to the A2990, the Old Thanet Way.

The divide between Whitstable and Tankerton seems to be at Tankerton Circus. On the map this area is called Kingsdown Park, though whether that counts as a district of Whitstable or Tankerton is unclear. I wonder if Tankerton Circus could be named for an old circus site. I delve into the dictionary and discover that circus is defined as “a travelling company of entertainers… a public performance given by such a company… an oval or circular arena, usually tented and surrounded by tiers of seats, in which such a performance is held…”. But it can also be “an open place, usually circular, in a town, where several streets converge.”[2] And that exactly describes Tankerton Circus. Its centre is a roundabout planted with shrubs, palm trees, and cacti from which radiate six exits – one for Kingsdown Park East, one for Kingsdown Park West and two each for Tankerton Road and St. Anne’s Road.

During my time at the Little Blue Hut, I only become familiar with Marine Parade (the coastal road) and the eastern part of Tankerton Road. These are connected by the northern part of St Anne’s Road. St Anne’s – the name takes me back to my childhood and the seaside holidays we had at my grandparents’ Lancashire home. This road is flanked by tennis courts on either side mostly used by retired folk enjoying extra ‘leisure’ time.

Marine Parade runs the whole length of Tankerton’s stretch of coast. I park my car at its western end each time I come to the Little Blue Hut. It has buildings only on one side so all command excellent sea views. Many of the houses have been designed to make the most of the situation with sitting rooms on upper floors, wide windows and balconies. *The Marine Hotel* and *The Royal* provide places to eat, drink and stay but most of the properties are privately owned with new ones being built. An excavator digs up a plot of land in preparation for an extension to a residential home. One penthouse flat is for sale at £800,000 – an exorbitant amount for East Kent. Next to *The Marine Hotel* are *Tankerton Grand Mansions* with Art Deco style decoration, an arch over the entrance to their car park and incredibly tall chimneys which suggest these flats were once truly grand.

The houses and bungalows are in varying styles and from different eras. Long before the residency I would 'tortoise' to Marine Parade – when things are too noisy or pre-occupying at home, I jump in the car and drive off somewhere. Once parked up, I lay the front passenger seat flat to use as a desk and spread my papers and books out. Somehow, in a different place, with a different vista, my horizons change and creativity flows. One day parked up near number 73, this poem emerged:

A House Marks Time

I'm parked outside number seventy-three
and though it looks nothing like the house I grew up in
that is where it takes me.

And I'm wondering if like a Narnian wardrobe
I can touch the door handle, push it open
and find myself transported

to my tiny bedroom above the kitchen
with my father's voice rising: Isn't she up yet?
which I'm foolishly ignoring

trying to laze and stretch in my too-narrow bed
turning over what it might be like
if he were dead.

I'm in that place
and number seventy-three
no longer holds me.

The poem was published in *inc. magazine, issue* 5.[3] The issue's theme was place and the editors creatively converted each poem into a postcard. Mine was illustrated by Reena Makwana. Number 73 on Marine Parade is a bungalow with dormer window, white pebble-dash and tall chimney; nothing like my 1970 square-box home. The illustrator chose Number 73 to be a terraced house – I guess there are as many versions of '73' as there are streets of sufficient length.

My favourite house on Marine Parade is *Peggotty House.* It is unique with a curving roof of small brown tiles and many tiny latticed windows including a couple of dormers. The walls are white with wooden beams, or tiny bricks in interesting patterns. At the front the upper storey overhangs the lower and is propped up by five wooden struts creating a walkway along the house. It has a dolls-house-grown-large appearance and is set to one side of its grounds. These are laid to lawn and planted with bordering shrubs. A white wall topped with ivy separates the front garden from the rear and attaches the house to the garage which has similar lattice windows in brown wooden doors. Very recently the house went up for sale and I quickly investigated the estate agent's website. But at £900,000 it is way beyond my price range. More sadly it's advertised with "there may be potential to build an additional dwelling or to significantly extend the existing house".[4] I doubt that *Peggotty House* will remain so charming in the future.

I wonder if the house is named after Peggotty in David Copperfield. She was kind to David, a homely sort of person, which fits with this house's architecture. Dickens connections extend along the Kent coast. He wrote *David Copperfield* and began *Bleak House* whilst staying at Fort House in Broadstairs. This he rented every summer for 22 years. Its name was changed to Bleak House after his death. On Broadstairs' seafront is Dickens House, set out as a museum to the great writer. It was owned by Mary Pearson Strong on whom Dickens based the character of Betsey Trotwood – another Copperfield connection. Each year Broadstairs holds a Dickens week with costumed walks and performances of his work. Rochester also holds an annual Dickens Festival. Dickens lived in Rochester and Chatham, incorporating many of the buildings of Chatham High Street into his novels.

Marine Parade stretches into Marine Crescent – more large houses with lovely views. But there is a spot for those with lesser budgets. Beyond Marine Crescent, heading towards the marshes of the Swale estuary, is a short un-named road. On its shore side is a patch of grass and a large building hidden by trees. This is Lang Court, a sheltered housing complex. I've been inside several times as it was home to a poetry friend who held readings in the Court's lounge until she died. The road is a favourite stop for motorhome owners who make the most of free parking to enjoy the coastal location. Year round you can see two or three, maybe more, parked up. Only the very coldest weather seems to deter them.

Tankerton Road runs parallel to Marine Parade and is the main retail street for Tankerton. I frequent *Tesco Metro, Ossie's Fish and Chips* and the café, *89,* but there is also *The Wine Room, Flex Appeal Gym, Graystone Bags, Woollard and Kent Funeral Services,* a pharmacy, takeaways, restaurants, several charity, gift and 'corner' shops, a baker's and a betting shop. In the middle of this run stands a charming bungalow, which catches the eye, not only because it is a house among shops, but also because it has stone models of a manor house and a castle inhabiting the front patio alongside large planted tubs.

Tankerton began as a commercial development of the estates of Tankerton Tower and was originally called Tankerton-on-Sea.

The 'Lord of the Manor' still controls building regulations and access rights along the backs of the houses. The current 'lords' are John and Keith Bishop.[5] Some of the road names reflect the Tower's history. There are Graystone, Wynn and Ellis Roads.

Swalecliffe is named from the old English words *swalwe* meaning a swallow and *clif* meaning an escarpment or hill-slope. It appears in the Domesday Book as Soaneclive. The parish church is dedicated to Saint John the Baptist. Saxon and Norman churches have occupied the site but the present Grade II listed building was created in Gothic style in 1875. At that time the population was 168 with only 32 houses including the rectory. Swalecliffe also boasted a "slightly endowed" school and a coastguard station.

The railway first stopped at Swalecliffe Halt in 1930 as part of the London, Chatham and Dover Railway's London Victoria to Dover Line.[6] The station is now known as Chestfield and Swalecliffe (Chestfield being a larger village to the south of Swalecliffe) and is a 'station stop' on Southeastern's Ramsgate to Victoria service.

I don't do much exploration of Tankerton or Swalecliffe, just the occasional walk. I am absorbed by sea and shore. However, I do discover more about Tankerton Slopes.

Slope Dwellers

Inclined: adj. ***1*** *having a disposition; tending.*
2 *sloping or slanting*[1]

Most days of my residency I walk from the hut in one direction or the other – whether west or east I tend to keep to the shore, enjoying the sounds and sights of the lapping sea, becoming more intrigued by the habits of birds and people, more aware of the tides, the colours of sea and sky, and the vegetation. One sunny afternoon, I stop and stare at a cormorant with outstretched wings, nosy at people and gulls on the beach, until splat. I slide onto my bottom down a wet slipway. Ouch! Yuk! I'm covered with slimy green weed.

I need a treat. I head up the slope at its eastern end to go to *The Seaview Café*.[2] They're doing a brisk business in late lunches, afternoon teas and ice-creams. I buy a *Mr Whippy* topped with a flake and decide to walk back to the hut along the top of the slope.

Grass runs the length of the seaward side of Marine Parade. In winter it's often boggy – a reminder that this is reclaimed marshland – but at present the grass is dry and green. Usually it's occupied by a few dog-walkers and a couple of people sitting on the benches. Most of these seats bear plaques in memory of somebody who loved the place. My favourite:

IN MEMORY OF
CHARLES MARTIN TWIST
REST IN PEACE
FROM ALL YOUR LOVED ONES

Did they really give him such a hard time? He certainly wouldn't find much peace if he was here today. The grass is littered with people on deckchairs, rugs and benches, munching sandwiches and sausage rolls, licking lollies and ice-creams, slurping drinks from bottles and flasks, dozing, reading or filling in puzzle magazines. The sun has brought out a flock of folk who haven't the inclination to go all the way to the beach. They've either parked up on Marine Parade or walked to the top and stopped, made nests, and are quietly enjoying the afternoon, for though I intimated that Mr Twist wouldn't find much peace, there isn't any raucous behaviour, not even a family game of football or French cricket.

These slope dwellers are divided into two breeds. Sea-Devotees site their chairs for views of shore, sea and beyond, though any White Lady Worshippers must be disappointed. The turbines are veiled by a mauve haze. Sun-Soakers face south for maximum exposure. They stay unaware of the tide's ebb and flow and would be oblivious to an approaching alien invasion. Actually, there's a third category – Huddlers. These sit in little circles doling food from a cool-box, cups of tea from a flask, snippets of news from papers, laced with their opinions – a transfer of their usual home activities, minus the TV, to the sunshine of the slope.

These people are well-served with public toilets and cafés. For any who want to reach the beach, concrete paths and steps criss-cross the incline. These are enjoyed by children on scooters who rattle and bump all the way to the bottom or until courage runs out resulting in a foot put down or a panicked jump-off. The paths are paced by fitness fanatics keen to improve aerobic capacity, and a unicyclist measures his mastery by how far he cycles before losing his balance. He repeatedly aims for the top. When he succeeds, he pedals on to Marine Parade and away…

The beach huts perch on the slope, arranged in three blocks. My hut is at the edge of the westernmost set. The two other groups are either side of Tankerton Bay Sailing Club's clubhouse.[3] This dark wood-clad building has good views out to sea. Surrounding it, as you might guess, lie sailing dinghies, catamarans and other craft whose rigging sings on a windy day. Also on the slope, housed within a converted beach hut, are the headquarters for Whitstable Coastwatch.[4] The National Coastwatch is a voluntary organisation begun in 1994 after two fishermen drowned off Cornwall near the site of a recently closed coastguard station. Whitstable, one of 49 stations that now exist around Britain, reports to the Thames coastguard service.

I often sit on the slope's grass near my hut. Others do the same whether hut owners or not. It's a peaceful place. A young couple rests from pushing tiny twins in a pair of buggies. The parents look remarkably well considering the sleepless nights they must be enduring – one at a time was enough for me. A man scrapes rust from his old deckchair before settling in it to watch and snooze. And a photographer takes pictures of the sea but then drops to his knees to capture bugs in the grass.

At the slope's western end is a small patch of woodland which is mainly composed of sycamore trees, but also has ash, holly, hawthorn, grey poplar and blackthorn. This has protected status as it's the largest area of mature woodland in Whitstable.[5] The majority of Tankerton Slopes is grassy, a mixture of long and short, with some shrubs and scrub vegetation. It provides rich pickings for the crows, gulls, pigeons, starlings and pipits. One day whilst writing in my hut I'm suddenly aware of a mechanical drone. The grass-cutters have come. Three men on machines methodically make their way along the slope shearing its summer coat.

Grass cutting releases a host of flies which buzz and bash at the hut's windows. They remind me of the couple of days when crane flies littered the grass surrounding the hut. I've been fascinated by daddy-longlegs for as long as I can remember. It wasn't the usual cruel childhood fascination for removing legs, but fuelled by Jean Webster's delightful novel *Daddy-Long-Legs*.[6] The copy I own is an old, cloth-bound hardback published by Hodder & Stoughton. I guess it might have been my mother's before becoming mine. The story has nothing to do with the insect but with a benefactor of long-legged stature who enables an orphanage girl to get a university education. I think my childish mind must have linked a human daddy-longlegs' goodness with a benign, appealing insect.

I remember daddy-longlegs flying through open windows on warm summer evenings. Ted Hughes poem, *A Crane Fly in September*,[7] gives the impression they are "past their time":

> She is struggling through grass-mesh – not flying,
> Her wide-winged, stiff, weightless basket-work of limbs
> Rocking, like an antique wain, a top-heavy ceremonial cart
> Across mountain summits…

But I saw the slope's daddy-longlegs in October. I ponder whether the unseasonal sunshine means they've survived longer – a thought which reveals my ignorance about their life cycle. Adult crane flies only live for a few days. They emerge from pupal cases, mate and lay eggs in grassy ground within twenty-four hours. After gestating for about two weeks, larvae hatch. These are leatherjackets, named for their grey/brown leathery skin. They are sensitive to drying out, so remain underground feeding on roots through the day. At night, when the grass is damp, they rise to eat shoots. But in a wet, mild autumn they can be on the surface most of the time – a nightmare for lovers of a manicured lawn. Birds and small mammals add to the dishevelment by pecking and digging up turf to feed on the larvae feast. Leatherjackets chomp all through autumn, winter and spring. They generally pupate in May or June and the crane flies emerge in July or August to start the mating and egg laying ritual again.[8]

So daddy-longlegs do belong to summer evenings. Why did I see them around the beach hut in October? Climate change, it seems, is affecting crane flies causing them to emerge later in the year – a strategy to avoid being a significant food source for birds and bats. Crane flies are not yet endangered but continued housing development and intensive agriculture affects their chances of survival. They need grassland. There are 350 species of crane fly in Britain, of which 20 were unknown here before the 1980s and three of these were previously undiscovered species.[9] In towns, often brownfield sites are the only suitable habitats left for crane flies. So it's pleasing to find Tankerton Slopes provide a home for my favourite childhood insect.

In fact, Tankerton Slopes is a designated SSSI.[10] Though not the haunt of some super-duper Secret Service, the slopes are scrutinised for intruders and potential destruction, whether malicious or from ignorance. The acronym identifies a Site of Special Scientific Interest, a designation given by Natural England, not because of the crane flies but, because the Slopes sustain a very rare creature; one that I never see.

The Fisher's Estuarine Moth has only two homes in Britain – the National Nature Reserve at Walton-on-the-Naze in Essex and here on Tankerton Slopes. Like most moths, it is a night flier, with a wingspan of about 4-6cm. It is pale orange-brown in colour, with dark and light spots and a dark band on the lower forewings. The adults fly in September and October. The species overwinters as eggs which the moths lay in coarse grass. There are plenty of places in Britain that could provide such habitat. Their rarity is due to the food requirements of the caterpillars which live from June to August.[11] They have only one food source, initially feeding on the stems and, later, the roots. Fisher's Estuarine Moths needs hog's fennel, a relatively rare coastal plant but one which flourishes on Tankerton Slopes.

Hoar Strange, Brimstonewort…

…sulphurwort or hoar strong are all names, according to Dr Culpeper, for hog's fennel. Sulphur and brimstone could be due to the odour of its thick roots. If wounded in spring, they release a yellowish-green juice which dries to a sulphurous-smelling resin. Hoar is less obvious – the leaves, divided into long narrow segments, are maybe reminiscent of hoarfrost. And hog? Perhaps once upon a time hogs inhabited the same marshland. Hog's fennel is related to the vegetable fennel but hog's fennel leaves are less feathery and its flowers are larger.

Hog's fennel is rare – actually, very rare. Though native to Britain, hog's fennel is only found in two places, either side of the Thames estuary, at Walton-on-the-Naze in Essex and along the north Kent coast from Faversham to Reculver. It likes salt marsh conditions, needing some soil salinity, but cannot survive on land that is encroached by the sea. So Tankerton Slopes are ideal and each summer these tall plants (they grow up to 2 metres) with woody stems, show off their yellow umbels.[1]

Umbel – I know this is a flower word, but I'm unsure of its precise meaning. It seems suggestive of umbrellas and the heads of flowers on hog's fennel do look a bit like upside-down umbrellas. I hunt out a definition:

> **Umbel:** an inflorescence, characteristic of umbelliferous plants, in which the flowers arise from the same point in the main stem and have stalks of the same length, to give a cluster with the youngest flowers at the centre. [c.16 from Latin umbrella, a sunshade, from umbra shade.][2]

My umbrella notion was right. Hog's fennel is classified as an umbellifer. These have hollow stems, divided leaves and flowers in umbels. Umbellifers include carrot, parsley, parsnip and celery which also have wild coastal versions. Only hog's fennel is rare. Alexanders, another yellow-flowering umbellifer but with broader leaves divided as trefoils, and other marshland plants compete with hog's fennel on Tankerton Slopes. As part of the SSSI monitoring these may be cleared so the hog's fennel can flourish.

Nowadays hog's fennel is prized for its connection with the Fisher's Estuarine Moth but Nicholas Culpeper suggested in *The English Physitian*:

> the juice used with vinegar and rose-water, or with a little Euphorbium put to the nose benefits those that are troubled with the lethargy, frenzy or giddiness of the head, the falling sickness, long and inveterate

> headache, the palsy, sciatica and the cramp, and generally all the diseases of the sinews, used with oil and vinegar. The juice dissolved in wine and put into an egg is good for a cough or shortness of breath, and for those that are troubled with wind. It also purgeth gently and softens hardness of the spleen.... A little of the juice dissolved in wine and dropped into the ears or into a hollow tooth easeth the pains thereof. The root is less effectual to all the aforesaid disorders, yet the powder of the root cleanseth foul ulcers, and taketh out splinters of broken bones or other things in the flesh and healeth them perfectly; it is of admirable virtue in all green wounds and prevents gangrene. [3]

A wonderful cure-all. Perhaps it grew more abundantly in the 17th century. Culpeper claimed it was plentiful in the salt marshes near Faversham. Even earlier, in 1597, the Jesuit Priest, John Gerard, lists hog's fennel in his *Herball or Generall Historie of Plantes*. This was an epic tome running to 1480 pages of descriptions and illustrations. The *Herball* mentions hog's fennel growing in the same two areas, around Faversham and Walton, "in a meadow neere to the seaside".[4]

I'm a novice when it comes to plant identification. As children, my sisters and I were encouraged to pick specimens of flowers on country walks. At home we laid them between sheets of blotting paper which were placed within the volumes of *Encyclopaedia Britannica.* Once dried, we mounted the flowers in scrapbooks adding identifying labels. I loved turning those large, grey, thick pages and examining each specimen in turn. Pressed flowers lose colour intensity but their increased fragility kindled my sense of wonder. I still enjoy pressing flowers but only choose ones from my garden or use fallen petals. I remember a few of those childhood plants, but only a very few, and they are countryside rather than coastal species. It's a case of neglected knowledge is soon forgotten. Even in my garden, I know only a minority of the plant names – marigolds, cornflowers, the buddleia bush, and the spring bulbs. I've been happy to admire without needing to classify.

My renewed interest is sparked by the discovery of a yellow-flowering poppy-like plant. I know the red poppies of wheat fields and war memorials. They grow on single stems but these are in clumps on the shingle. I discover they are yellow horned-poppies. These inhabit shingle or sandy locations, particularly in south-east England.[5] They are named for their flower colour and for their seed pods which can be up to 30cm long and are curved, looking like miniature elephant tusks. Before the seeds are ready for dispersal, the pods cling tenaciously to the plant but once mature they easily snap off the stem and a simple twist reveals many tiny seeds.[6]

Yellow horned-poppy extract shares some of the narcotic properties associated with other poppies. The extract, glaucine, apparently has similar effects as codeine and can give "pleasant feelings of great exaltation and euphoria". A website which gives detailed information about who should and shouldn't use yellow horned-poppy extract and its possible side effects, also categorically states:

INFORMATION PROVIDED ON OUR WEBSITE IS FOR BOTANICAL/CULTURAL RESEARCH PURPOSES ONLY! ANY REFERENCES ABOUT THE USE OR EFFECTS OF THESE NATURAL HEALING HERBS IS BASED ON TRADITIONAL USE OR SHAMANIC PRACTICES. ALL

PRODUCTS ARE SOLD FOR ETHNOBOTANICAL RESEARCH (NOT FOR HUMAN CONSUMPTION)!!! (Their capitals and punctuation.)[7]

Yellow horned-poppy was once thought to be beneficial when applied to bruises, hence its alternative names of bruiseroot and squatmore (a squat being a bruise).[8]

A poppy grows upon the shore
 Bursts her twin cup in summer late:
Her leaves are glaucous green and hoar,
 Her petals yellow, delicate.

from **A Sea Poppy by Robert Bridges**[9]

Robert Bridges' poem provides a lovely description of the yellow horned-poppy. Its grey-green leaves have wavy edges and its flowers have large, delicate petals. On the day we met she wasn't shivering and forlorn, as he suggests later in the poem, but seemed to bask in and reflect the sun. She certainly made me a lover. Yellow horned-poppies generally bloom from July to September so I was lucky to discover a plant still bearing flowers. These poppies incite my curiosity to learn more about other plant species. But that's not so easy. Most poppy clumps are without their flowers and the hog's fennel is beginning to die back. Other plants have no flowers, are losing leaves and dying down. Autumn's not the best time to begin my education.

I find one plant with pink flowers, another with yellow, still in bloom. The yellow ones look like a variation on a dandelion and, aided by a friend, I eventually identify them as hawksbeard.[10] These aren't typically coastal plants but there is a marshland variety. My flower guide says marsh hawksbeard grows in dry sandy places which would explain its position in the shingle bordering the promenade. It has orange-yellow composite flowers so each has many petals. The stems are almost hairless and the leaves are pointed, yellow-green, shiny and shallowly toothed.

The pink flowers are problematic, and it is not until the following summer, when I see them again, that I become certain of their identity. Confusingly, for the flowers are very pink, they are red valerian. This is a greyish-green perennial with oval-shaped untoothed leaves which straddle the stem in opposite pairs. The flowers are tiny – 8-10mm long but are clustered together to form dense terminal heads. I spotted red valerian poking up amongst the huge rocks placed as erosion protection. Valerian prefers broken rocky ground, chalk cliffs and old walls and though not native is now widely naturalised.[11] And once I have identified it, guess what happens? I see red valerian in many coastal places including clinging to the chalk cliffs by the steps from the promenade to the beach at Ramsgate.

The only other species which I manage to identify whilst on my residency are sea kale and sea beet. Neither is still in bloom, but the sea kale's cabbage-like leaves make it relatively easy to recognise and the sea beets sprawl and still have their spikes of fruit. Sea kale has smooth, fleshy, crinkly-edged, silvery-green leaves and its tiny white flowers bloom from June to August.[12] It is edible: the leaves can be used as salad or cooked as vegetable; the roots contain more starch than potatoes and some protein; the stems taste mildly of pea and cabbage; the fragrant flowers make a tasty garnish for meat and fish. It was preserved in barrels to take on board boats in Roman times as its high vitamin C content prevented scurvy. Sea kale has been cultivated in Europe from the 1600s. But before you rush off to forage, I should warn that it's illegal to harvest. A penchant for its flavour and appearance meant many were uprooted from our coasts in Victorian times, and transplanted into vegetable growers' plots and ornamental gardens. Increased sea-defences have further reduced places in which colonies of sea kale grow and unaware walkers sometimes trample and kill young shoots.[13]

Sea beet has dark green, hairless, shiny leaves which are triangular and wavy near the base of the plant and narrower towards the ends of stems. The flowers are also green and grow in narrow spikes. As the fruits develop they often stick together in a prickly mass. Both beetroot and sugar beet are cultivated versions.[14] Sea beet is common in many coastal locations. I find tangles of it on the shingle looking like discarded wigs of matted orange-brown locks.

The following summer I return to Tankerton Slopes. Many plants are in bloom, so with camera and plant guide in hand, I continue to learn. The area has two main habitats – the shingle and the grassy marshland – both of which provide species to identify. I discover common mallow plants with their lobed leaves and pink 5-petalled flowers, veined with purple. They decorate the edge of the promenade, rooted into the shingle. I also find sea carrot, ragwort, sea bindweed, sea lavender, shore dock and mugwort. It's so exciting to be able to convert pictures in a book to the reality of living plants. Hidden under the platform of a beach hut I spot the wonderful seed heads of a goatsbeard. And another day, nearer to home at Pegwell Nature Reserve, I find sea holly. This has to be one of my favourites. Sea holly will only survive where the sand is unstable. It's a perennial and creeps along the ground, reaching a height of 30-60cm. Its blue-green spiky leaves have white veins and look like a ghostly version of ordinary holly leaves. In July and August it displays minute blue flowers crammed together in a globular head. Once seen and named, it is one of those plants that can't be forgotten.[15]

Despite having made some progress I still feel ignorant about flower species of coastal regions (and countryside too). But I am encouraged to keep on learning. I wonder if the Brent geese were pecking eelgrass – one of their favourite foods. Eelgrass grows where it will be covered by the incoming tide but it is rooted in the mud so is not washed away.[16] One afternoon at low tide I explore 'the green' where I'd seen the geese feeding. It covers a large area of the shingle in short fronds, but is easily separated from the stones. It doesn't have roots – it must be some kind of seaweed.

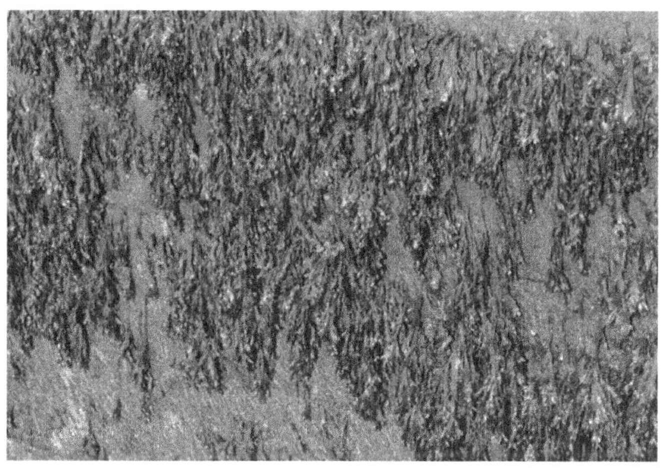

Holdfasts for Bladder, Gut and Belt

This chapter isn't about medical supports for saggy bits or appliances to keep us upright. Holdfasts are parts of seaweeds, not scientific inventions. Mind you, seaweeds are supposed to provide miracle cures for cancer and have excellent anti-inflammatory and bug-fighting properties. It's claimed they aid metabolism, revitalise our bodies, provide iodine for healthy thyroid function and are effective in treating wounds, burns and rashes. Seaweeds have been food and medicine since the Romans ruled Europe, and from prehistoric times in Chinese, Japanese and Korean cultures.[1]

I know less about seaweed than I do about coastal flowers. I'd noticed remnants lying on the strandline and various seaweeds revealed at low tide, but at the beginning of my residency I'm so absorbed by other things – sea, birds, tides, moon, to name a few – that seaweed doesn't really register on my radar. An idea for a poem sparks my interest. Usually the reverse occurs – some discovery ignites creativity. But as I watched a woman walk along the promenade dressed head-to-toe in black, clothes far too warm for the sunny day, the phrase widow's weeds dropped into my mind. I began to imagine a lady who makes clothes from gathered seaweed. To write, I must research.

Seaweed is a catch-all name for thousands of species of marine algae. They vary from tiny microscopic filaments to abundant 'forests'. Algae are simple plants in the evolutionary chain. They don't flower. Instead they have a reproductive cycle with alternating forms – a microscopic stage is followed by the seaweed spore-forming stage. With no xylem and phloem internal transport systems, they rely on simple uptake into cells from their surroundings. They don't have roots. Holdfasts, which look like roots, are for holding fast. They anchor seaweed to a rock, shell or stone but can't absorb nutrients or water.[2]

Seaweeds, like flowering plants, create food by photosynthesis and contain the necessary green pigment, chlorophyll. They are classified according to colour: green (about 1500 different species), brown (about 1800 species) and red (an amazing 6500 species).[3] All have chlorophyll but the phycoerythrin pigment in red seaweeds and fucoxanthin in brown species mask the green. Seaweeds have fronds instead of leaves. These have one of three basic constructions: a slender filament, a network of thin branches or a broad, flat lamina. Many species live in the intertidal zones and are adapted to survive submersion in water and exposure to air.

I first spot three different seaweeds: bright green filaments decorating the groynes and covering the stones near where the geese peck; another green species, with flattened lamina and crinkly edges, splayed along the clay at low tide; and a greenish-brown kind with branching fronds complete with pods.

The green filaments: I decide this is gutweed (*Ulva intestinalis*).[4] Its simple tubular fronds are only one cell thick and up to seven centimetres long. It is aptly named; the fronds have randomly spaced constrictions so they look like some alien's gut. It's found near the top of the shore as it can survive frequent exposure to air, and often forms a slippery carpet. Ah ha! Gutweed was the cause of my slide down the slipway. It's edible – either as salad or boiled as a vegetable. Shredded and fried it's the crispy seaweed of Chinese dishes.

Flat green fronds: this must be sea lettuce (*Ulva lactus*) I've only seen the odd splodge of these fronds, but it can form a slippery carpet on rocks near the shoreline. It also grows on the middle and lower shore as swaying 'forests' in rock pools. Its irregular bright green fronds, often tattered, resemble lettuce leaves. Sea lettuce can be eaten in salads and soups.

Greenish-brown, branching with pods: I see this clinging to the groynes, to the concrete surrounding the rainwater run-off pipes and to the harbour wall. I decide it's probably bladderwrack (*Fucus vesiculosus*). Bladderwrack can hybridise with other varieties which can make identification difficult. The pods are air-filled bladders that act as floats when the tide comes in. There are many types of wrack – the one I've spotted could be serrated wrack. This has branching fronds with a midrib and serrated edges. It develops swollen reproductive structures at the frond tips in winter. But apparently serrated wrack is rarely found in the south-east, so I plump for bladderwrack.

Deciding which seaweed is which is difficult. I'm acutely aware of limited knowledge. I tend to operate on rare things are seen rarely and, when in doubt, choose a species that is common. I'm not sure that my identification of bladderwrack is correct – but it's definitely some kind of wrack.

A greater variety of seaweeds is found at two locations near the hut: The Street and the area of shingle between Tankerton and Swalecliffe known as Long Rock. These are great to explore at a spring tide when the water recedes to its lowest ebb. I discover many seaweeds. Most I just identify as red, brown or green but some I succeed in naming:

Kelps are brown seaweeds: oarweed (*Laminaria digitalis*) has fronds divided into broad, strap-like segments; sea belt (*Saccharina latissima*) grows as a flat broad frond with crinkly edges and has a narrow stipe or stem; furbelows (*Saccorhiza polyschides*) have many-divided long fronds; and dabberlocks (*Alaria esculenta*) have long fronds with a midrib and delicate blade. All are impressive. Laid out flat on the spit they look ready for the picking but if you bend and pull, a holdfast keeps them anchored.

Dulse (*Palmaria palmate*) is a red seaweed which attaches to rocks or to kelp stipes. The multi-branched fronds are a rosy-purplish colour which deepens through the summer. Its urn-shaped female receptacles are found in the forks of the branches. It's a well-known edible seaweed though it can be rather salty and tough.

A delicate red seaweed with tiny feathery fronds could be *Jania Rubens* which is less rigid than its look-a-like coralweed but I'm not sure – the guidebook suggests both species are rare on the north Kent coast.

Not all seaweeds are still held-fast. Some are scattered along the strandline, often dried out, crisp and black. When I found my name engraved in the concrete of the harbour arm, it was hidden amongst bound lobster claws and blackened seaweed – a wrack of some kind with long stringy fronds and egg-shaped bladders. It could be egg wrack (*Ascophyllum nodosum*). Or maybe not. Again, the guidebook says it's uncommon in SE England.

I remain a novice. Maybe one day I'll take the plunge and sign up for a coastal discovery day or a foraging course. These seem to be increasing in popularity and a few hours with an expert might furnish me with more knowledge than days spent wandering, guidebook in hand. I find one advertised at Deal on the South Kent coast. This also has a shingle beach so the seaweed species might be similar.

Seaweed is nutritious food if you know the right ones to pick, and commercially it is used in many products from shampoo to face creams, from setting agents to animal feed to fertilisers. For a time I cultivated an allotment in Ramsgate. Each year the council dumped tractor-loads of seaweed on site which we greedily forked into our compost heaps. Thanet beaches suffer with more washed-up seaweed in the summer than most other places in the country – 6000-7000 tonnes in comparison to an average 900 tonnes.[5] The soft chalk reef which surrounds the majority of the coastline provides excellent anchorage for holdfasts. More growth means more to be washed ashore. For Blue Flag status, the beaches are cleared of deposited seaweed. Some becomes good manure.

As seaweed novice, I create my poem, written in elegiac couplets – an ancient Greek form used for funeral songs.[6]

Sea Weeds

Daily she gathers armfuls of bladderwrack, carries them home,
dries until black, then weaves fronded weeds for her love.

Yet she fetches sea lettuce and gutweed to feed on their juices
resourcing strengths, awaiting the dawn of mourning's end.

This poem is fanciful, weird. But then, truth is often stranger than fiction.

There's nowt so queer as folk

excepting thee and me,
and I'm not too sure about thee.[1]

People are fascinating. No matter how ordinary they look, sound or act, every person has a twist in their tale – something that makes them unique. Though I'm absorbed by sea, sky, shore and slope, people still catch my attention. Why have they come? What's brought them to this place on the same day and at the same time as me? If we played six degrees of separation would we discover connections other than geography?

Tankerton Slopes differ from a town centre or industrial estate in that most people are here because they've chosen to visit for leisure and pleasure – maybe they're regulars, so coming is part of their normal routine, or maybe their visit is a treat, a break from their usual lives, perhaps marking some special occasion.

A few are here to work:

One of the first people I photograph is a rubbish collector wheeling his metal trolley piled high with Day-Glo orange sacks that match his high-vis jacket. He trundles along the promenade from one bin to the next replacing full sacks with new ones and picking up litter with his long-handled grabber. Is his job more enjoyable for being able to walk along the shore?

The grass cutters are also high-vis men, one of whom takes time to toss pebbles into the sea before climbing aboard his mower. I presume they're council men or sub-contractors. Where and what else fills their days?

In autumn, the lifeguards are only employed at weekends – a boy and girl, dressed in the same bright red and yellow as their hut, open up and set out their high-chair and sea-canoe. They take flags, one each to east and west, to plant as boundary markers of their watch.

The lifeguards are part of Foreshore Services whose vans regularly patrol the promenade. One day in October, two vans stop. Men jump out, dismantle and load up the lifeguard hut, and take it away for winter hibernation.

And me. Do I classify as a worker?

As part of my contract I've agreed to be in residence for at least eighteen days during my designated six weeks. So, I have some obligation. I write, contemplate, learn and create which require time and energy commitment. But I'm not paid (other than with free use of the hut which at Whitstable rates counts for quite a lot) and there are no definite outcomes to measure – I won't have emptied so many rubbish bins, sheared so much grass, kept watch over people's lives.

Except I have kept watch. I spend a considerable amount of my time observing people as they pass by or stop to settle on the beach. I've also eavesdropped (unintentionally, of course). I feel a bit like Baudelaire's flâneur[2] but of the coast instead of the city. I'm both an outsider looking in and a participant in the scene. When L.S. Lowry, the artist, moved into industrial Lancashire he was at first appalled by his surroundings. But slowly he became fascinated and then addicted to painting them.

> I saw the industrial scene and I was affected by it. I wanted to get a certain effect on the canvas. I couldn't describe it, but I knew it when I'd got it.[3]

Far be it from me to bracket myself with Lowry but alongside my growing awareness, curiosity and love for this place is a desire to insert its people into my creativity whether they are inhabitant or visitor. Actually, everyone's a visitor to the sea and shore. There aren't any human residents of the shingle. My hut's wide windows encourage the notion of being inside a wildlife hide. I begin to record some 'bird' families.

A flamingo dad wearing bright orange trousers arrives by bike with his duckling son dressed all in yellow strapped into a carrier seat. They throw stones into the sea and over the groyne. The duckling waddles off to play his own games of jumping steps and stone fling-and-crash. A grey dove mother walks past with her chaffinch daughter and, on another day, a family of gulls arrives. Father and son come first – white chested, grey bottomed – they aim stones at the sea and Hi-five and cheer each time one plops in the water. The mother flies by on bicycle and almost misses them but the dad squawks loudly to bring her into land. Time and again I see dads creating rules of engagement for their particular version of the stone-throwing game. But I also notice how toddlers become absorbed in their own play; stacking and arranging, piling stones on the promenade, seeking out shells and enjoying crash'n'splash. Grown-ups become bored long before children are ready to leave.

One Wednesday it seems is grandparents' day – tiny tots are accompanied by older adults. Perhaps it's a general trend – my friend cares for her two grandchildren on a Wednesday. I make a note to check the following week. Theory unsubstantiated. No grandparent carers are out.

I watch families picnic, paddle and hunt for treasures. I also witness the power of an adult to pick up and carry when it's time to go. I mainly see toddlers, probably because I'm usually at the hut during school hours, but one day I'm treated to a delightful family of mother, father and three daughters. The eldest is on the cusp of adulthood but still enough of a girl to run and dart, her long hair flowing like a horse's mane; she wears the colours of sea and spray. With camera in hand she sets her family in different poses. She's a go-between – both adult and child respond to her liveliness and enthusiasm as she creates memories with games and photographs.

Many come to the beach to use the sea. Fishermen go out in boats from Whitstable harbour, set rods on stands balanced on the shingle or wander the spit in their waders. Fishermen mean lugworm-diggers are needed. They cross the mud at low tide with trademark bucket and fork. I see canoeists, wind-surfers, sailors, kite-surfers and water-skiers. All wait for the right conditions of tide and wind to indulge their passions.

And swimmers. I spoke to one on the equinox day who said it was the latest he'd ever swum in the English sea. But I see him again on later dates and others too, even into the middle of October. Some strip off to Speedos, race from groyne to groyne. Others play wearing colourful costumes, bikinis and shorts. One lady arrives in Lycra bottoms and red T-shirt, hair tied up in a bun. She stays in the water for quite some time bobbing and swirling – her chosen release from everyday routine.

One Monday morning several young women jog past; yummy-mums grabbing me-time after the weekend. The promenade is often blessed with exercise enthusiasts whether runners, walkers or cyclists. A man, dressed all in black, completes complicated routines with swirling stick and skipping rope. He faces the sea, perhaps daring to dream of some Canute-style capability. Another group of fitness fans bring their equipment to the top of the slope; claim that the good weather is saving them gym class fees.

I get out of my car one day and a man and his son flying their kite give me a bright 'Good morning' just as though we all meet here regularly. On another occasion, I'm trying my hand at kite-flying when an Eastern European guy stops to chat. His accent makes it difficult to decipher what he says. A while later I spot him and a friend preparing to kite-surf – inflating the edge of their huge kites, climbing into harnesses and wading out to sea, boards in hand. I guess he was giving helpful advice.

Walking and cycling have many purposes – to get from one place to another, for fitness, for enjoying fresh air and good scenery, for thinking things through, for chatting to friends. I reckon I see some people in all those categories and others who are harder to define. A lady, distinctive in turquoise cardigan and long skirt, pulls a shopping trolley. I later spot her sitting on a bench in Whitstable but with no evidence of having made any purchases. And a guy at the water's edge, dressed in colours of autumn, harvests something into a plastic carrier bag. From my hut he appears to disappear. Each time he bends down he's lost to view, only to rise again a few minutes later. He eventually strides up the slope and is gone.

Of course, dog-walkers abound – a huge range of people: the man in his Stetson controlling Labrador pups with a whistle; the girl dashing between the beach huts in pink fairy dress; the retired greyhounds with their retired humans. But the dog-lovers that particularly make me smile are not walkers at all. Both are owners of motorised wheelchairs. The first, a lady on a silver machine, zooms down the slope, one hand steering her chair and the other holding the lead of a little black dog. The dog strains at the leash, so my photograph conjures an image of him, a tiny thing, pulling her along.

The second, I nickname 'the monk' – not because he seems in any way religious but because, whatever the weather, he's covered in a navy waterproof from head to foot which looks rather like a habit. He owns three little dogs; one sits in a basket strapped to the handlebars, one on his lap and the third trots alongside. I wonder whether they swop around or if pack order ensures one dog never gets to ride.

A couple of people in wheelchairs make me feel more like a voyeur than flâneur, not because they are involved in anything sexual but because I witness some of their intimate difficulties. A white-haired lady in beige jacket is pushed by a younger relative or carer. They pause just below the hut. The carer steers the chair to face some railings and applies the brakes. The lady struggles, pulls herself up and walks a few steps clinging to the rail. But then the carer twists the chair so the lady can grab the handles. Chair turns into walking aid. She shuffles along the promenade.

Another day, towards the end of my residency, the sky is heavy with clouds. A couple arrive at the beach, she pushing him in a wheelchair. They stop at the edge of the path. She helps him out of the chair and with his hands resting on her shoulders, she walks backwards to guide him on to the beach. Part-way down, he rests on the groyne whilst she carries his chair so he can sit again. She then begins several journeys up and down the slope to fetch a chair for herself, a cool-box and book-filled bag, a windbreak and, when it starts to rain, coats and a gazebo. Her intimate care of his every need and their determination to make the most of their time at the beach, despite the scattered showers, are both inspiring and heart-rending.

How much each person treasures these surroundings, or how they cope with what life has furnished or thrown at them, is impossible to guess. Michael Blumenthal suggests in his poem, *What I Believe,*

> I believe we all drown eventually
> in a sea of our making,
> but that the land belongs to someone else.[4]

I don't chat with many people whilst on my residency; I don't really have insight into their lives. I hope they feel refreshed and restored from time by the sea. I also hope they are provoked to respect and care about nature. We've done so much to destroy our planet that it can feel like 'too-little-too-late'. Perhaps in re-connecting we will begin to find a less destructive way forward. Most of all, I hope they find this is a place where they can imagine and dream.

> I grow old… I grow old…
> I shall wear the bottoms of my trousers rolled.
>
> Shall I part my hair behind? Do I dare to eat a peach?
> I shall wear white flannel trousers, and walk upon the beach.
> I have heard the mermaids singing, each to each...
>
> We have lingered in the chambers of the sea
> By sea-girls wreathed with seaweed red and brown
> Till human voices wake us, and we drown.

from **'The Love Song of J. Alfred Prufrock'** by T.S. Eliot[5]

I shape-shift the people I see to create characters – the Leaf-turner, the Sea Sprite, the Unsettler... It becomes the stuff of poetry – heightened reality. I'm grateful to all those who provide the images which eventually pervade my work. And they're not all strangers – the friends who come for my Open Day transform into the Otherwise.

Open Day

Bellyful: as much as one wants or can eat.[1]

Chromatic: of, relating to, or characterised by a colour or colours.

Chromatography: the technique of separating and analysing the components of a mixture of liquid or gases by selective absorption in, for example, a column of powder or a strip of paper.[2]

Beyond the obligation to be at the Little Blue Hut at least eighteen times during my residency, my contract stipulates two further commitments: to hold an Open Day and to write a blog. I've blogged before but stopped when other writing became more consuming, and because I wasn't convinced anybody read my posts, other than one of my sisters, a couple of friends and every now and then, a hacker wanting to advertise their quirky habits or dodgy products. Still, my past experience means it's easy enough to set up a new one. I call it *Chromatography*, slightly twisting the dictionary definition: my residency pitch was based on colour in nature, and whilst here, I'm attempting some separation and analysis of my colour thoughts and ideas. It's fun to write short posts about my musings and illustrate them with photos. Last time I looked *Chromatography* was still out in blogosphere.[3]

An Open Day in autumn at a beach hut? The nature of the day is left open to interpretation so I decide to play safe and invite a select few. Then if the weather is atrocious, it won't be too cosy. I choose a Sunday near the end of the residency and send invitations for friends to come for a pot luck lunch and poetry workshop.

The week before, I begin preparations. Each time I come to the hut, I bring an extra chair, a rug, some more pens and paper… I even sweep the floor with a dustpan and brush. I shop for food and drink, paper plates and serviettes. I print out photos in A4 and A3 sizes and arrange them on the walls. That is satisfying: I discover I've captured a range of colours and the photos display the contrasts of the same place dressed in different 'clothes'. I also print off some small photos which I hope will act as writing prompts. After editing the few poems I've drafted, I put them into a file as proof of some achievement.

The day arrives. It's sunny. I needn't have worried. I pack my car with supplies and head for Marine Parade. I go early to ensure I will get a parking space on the stretch of road nearest to the hut. I'm already in party mood and as I start to unload, a cavalcade of old sports cars chugs past. There must be at least a dozen MGs revving and chuntering. With hoods down, the drivers are also glad of the autumn sun. I stand and stare, captivated by this other celebration.

Once at the hut, I dump my bags, open the shutters and start to rearrange the furniture to maximise space. I lay out my offerings of food and drink, and then step outside for a breather. A wolf walks up the slope. It must be an omen, though whether good or bad, I'm not sure. I guess it's some breed of dog, but with long-haired coat, pointed ears, sleek body, brush-like tail and no evidence of an owner, it appears more wolf than dog. I resist the urge to cry, "Wolf". Instead I take a photo as proof of its existence.

Just before noon, my guests start to arrive. One of the writing groups to which I belong is called the Bellyful, ostensibly because we enjoy a lot of poetry. Well, maybe that's only part of the story. Friends come laden with bags and baskets and soon my table is heaving with goodies. One or two have visited before but for the majority it's a new experience. They fall in love. There's hardly a cloud in the sky, a dozen white sailing dinghies race on a Delft blue sea, the Thames barge emerges from the harbour, sails furled but still magnificent, four swimmers splash and dash, and on the spit three sprites (sorry, men) fish.

My friends admire my photos but are more enchanted by the view. They wander down to the beach to throw pebbles in the water, sit outside or in, according to preference for sun or shade, enjoy the peace, but also keep watch on the ever-changing scene. I have fun using the hut as a hide to photo a photographer doing a shoot for an elegant young couple. They seem dressed for a posh restaurant or wedding reception, not a shingle beach. The man wears a navy blue, long-sleeved shirt with his collar buttoned up, and streamlined black trousers. She has a body-hugging, black-and-white, horizontally-striped dress, shimmering flesh-coloured tights and heels. Sharp, stiletto heels on smart black shoes. In contrast, the photographer wears jeans and a scruffy gilet. They parade the promenade, drape themselves around a beach hut and relinquish shoes to pose on the shingle. I take several photos, but the photographer must have captured so many more. I wonder whether they're for a business contract or for the couple's pleasure.

Back in the hut my friends pose for photos with notebooks and pencils in hand – evidence of the workshop. In reality, we never get round to writing, everybody is far too busy enjoying themselves. But they do take turns in reading out my poems. It's interesting to hear my work through different voices. I always read a poem aloud when I'm editing it and to perform them I learn by heart, which often makes me re-edit. But to hear others stumble over certain phrases or speak with an alternative rhythm, cadence or pronunciation, gives me a new perspective on each poem (and a desire for further editing).

After reading we troop outside for more photos. A spider lands on Jo and she becomes attached to the hut by a silken thread. Another omen? Let's hope it's a money spider. Spider silk, thickness for thickness, has the equivalent breaking strain of iron but is extremely light. A thread all around the world would weigh less than 150 grams. This delicate strength has been utilised in telescopic gun-sights.[4] In folklore, spider webs have healing properties. Such tales have stimulated investigation into their possible use in surgery. The silks are bio-compatible and bio-degradable so potentially could be suture threads or other implantable materials that need to be initially strong before being broken down by the body.[5]

For us, it just seems characteristic of Jo's fun nature that the spider chose her. In autumn, spiders 'balloon' as a quick way to get from one place to another. A spider climbs to a high point and turns to face the wind. Then it shoots several threads into the air which are caught by the breeze. The spider is lifted to a new location, hopefully one that is good for food. When large numbers of spiders balloon, the silk threads drift together and form gossamer. This appears as goose down on the ground and gossamer is thought to be a corruption of the phrase goose summer.[6]

Around four o'clock the Open Day closes, as many of us are due at a poetry event in Canterbury. It's been a great day, full of encouragement for me and hopefully inspiring to the others. I try to find a quote to sum up the experience. The best I come up with is:

> Some people go to priests; others to poetry; I to my friends, I to my own heart, I to seek among phrases and fragments something unbroken…[7]

This is from Virginia Woolf's *The Waves,* spoken by Bernard. The novel is related in the form of soliloquies by six different characters. Bernard's a storyteller,[8] something I also try to be through poetry. In some ways, the quote is apt. I'm glad of the support from the friends I've made on my writing journey. But I also appreciate poetry's input and gain much from my faith. Perhaps my quote should read:

> With faith, poetry and friends, my heart seeks among phrases and fragments for the unbroken, or for something to restore…

Poetry is concerned with metaphor and so the final words of the Open Day belong to the skein of geese that flies past as we are about to leave. Each goose has to flap its own wings, but as they fly together they conserve energy and find protection. This lot are a bit of a raggedy troop, no streamlined V formation, but together they have successfully accomplished the 2500-mile journey from Siberia.

From Long Rock to Hampton Bay

drift tales of smugglers, treachery,
of shifting sands, unstable clay,
a village drowned beneath the sea.

It's true! The village at the end of The Street may be mythical, but, as my verse relates, Hampton-on-Sea is a different kettle of fish. East of Swalecliffe, it originally consisted of a farmhouse, public house and a few wooden shacks made from bits of old boat and driftwood. Hampton-on-Sea's families, the Mounts and the Quicks, farmed, fished and supplemented their living by selling fossils and smuggling. The loss of Hampton-on-Sea is a cautionary tale of what can happen if man sets himself up as Nature's master.

Coastal erosion is a continual problem in this region. Remains of prehistoric and Roman habitations have been discovered in sites which are now offshore. Local farmers knew to keep watch and plant their crops at a suitable distance inland. But in 1864, *The Herne Bay, Hampton and Reculver Oyster Fishery Company* formed and an Act of Parliament gave the company rights to fish a six mile stretch of coast from Hampton to Reculver. Because of shallow coastal waters, a pier was built as a landing stage and shelter for the oyster smacks; it also acted as a breakwater for the breeding grounds.

The wood and concrete pier, completed in 1866, stretched 1,050 feet into the water with a slight westward curve. Do you remember that roving sailor, Longshore Drift? He wasn't too chuffed that an artificial barrier prevented the normal deposition of material. The flow tide dumped its load in front of the pier instead of carrying it to Hampton seafront. The pier also caused localised circular motion of the current to the west, which scoured out coastline soil. Hampton brook's tendency to flood, when spring tide, prolonged rainfall and onshore wind joined forces, became more frequent after the oyster company dug its fish pools. The combined result: acceleration of coastline erosion.

The oyster company didn't last. *HMS Buzzard* was posted to patrol the waters following disputes with other companies. During three severe winters in the 1870s, water froze in the breeding pools which killed the young oyster stock. By 1879 the company had gone into liquidation.

The oyster company built houses for its workers and a tramline to get the oysters to nearby Herne Bay station. But in 1879, Thomas Kyffin Freeman formed the *Hampton-on-Sea Estate Association* with the intention of developing a seaside resort. Unfortunately, he died in 1880 before he'd a chance to build much more than a bandstand. *The Land Company* bought the estate. They chartered trains from London and provided concerts, picnics and other entertainments as part of their marketing strategy. Advertisements suggested 'capitalists' could recoup investments by building small houses to let at large rents. 'Nature lovers' were tempted with a long list of fish to be caught and birds that could be shot!

Development began and terraced houses were constructed with good sea views – so good that the sea decided it didn't like such near neighbours. In 1898 part of the pier was removed and in 1899 a protecting wall built, but by the 1901 census several of the houses were uninhabitable with some already occupied by the sea. Most residents chose to move away, but one man, Edmund Reid, moved in. He was a colourful character, a former head of the Metropolitan Police, who bought 4, Eddington Gardens in 1903 and proceeded to paint its seaward wall with cannons and battlements. He raised the profile of the village by selling lemonade from his shed and postcards documenting the changing coastline. He eventually moved to Herne Bay in 1916, married, but died the following year.

Some houses fell into the sea, others were demolished, but by the mid-1930s the village of Hampton-on-Sea no longer existed. All that survives is Hampton Oyster Inn, now called Hampton Inn. It stands out clearly on the headland. Other houses have been built which are designated as part of Hampton, Herne Bay, but the land of the original Hampton-on-Sea is mainly underwater. Currently, there's a shortened pier and the coast is protected by imported rocks and a thick concrete wall.[1]

It's possible to walk from Tankerton to Hampton around the coast. So, one day, that's what I decide to do. A strong west wind blows, reminding me of Shelley's Ode:

O wild West Wind, thou breath of Autumn's being,
Thou, from whose unseen presence the leaves dead
Are driven, like ghosts from an enchanter fleeing…[2]

My walk's easy with the wind behind me but the black-headed gulls are having a hard time. As they attempt to fly on thermals, it seems their gearsticks are in reverse. Each time they rise they're forced backwards. They land, wait for another thermal and try again. Eventually persistence pays off; they angle their flight just right and soar beyond the shore. I walk the promenade, past the beach huts and the skateboard park where several lads with skateboards or BMXs practise tricks. I resist the temptation to buy something from the snack van strategically parked up to replenish their energy supplies, and continue onto the marshland. The tide's high so I stay on the paths rather than exploring the shingle. Swalecliffe brook meanders its way towards the sea, and the shingle and mud of Long Rock are gradually exposed as the tide ebbs.

I cross the brook at a small bridge and smile on reading the sign: "Naturism is not condoned on this beach". I can't see anybody flaunting the rule but back at home I discover that Long Rock is listed as a naturist beach on the Saturday Walkers' Club website.[3] I'm overtaken by a roller-blading lady who flies past as a vision of purple and black. She's heading for a rendezvous; later I see her perched against the seawall picnicking with a male friend.

A wide promenade takes me past the caravan site and follows the broad curve of the bay. Hampton Inn acts as a landmark and I pass other buildings, obviously further inland than the original Hampton-on-Sea, but still with good sea views. One home-owner has made the most of a flat roof by erecting an extra room on top, almost all of it window. Other houses stand tall so their upper storeys survey Essex on a clear day.

The beach feels somewhat desolate, perhaps because there are few people. Huge rusty pipes jut through and above the shingle. Presumably they're for rainwater. Maybe at one time they were covered by the stones but now they stick out round the bay, ugly and obtrusive. A solitary crow perches on one and next to him lies an empty Coke can. A sign says this is a *No Swim Zone* so I'm surprised to see a lady in the water. She could have been the twin of the roller-blader – this time a vision of pink and black. My imagination invents spies and secret missions…

Near Hampton, crows and gulls peck amongst the weed. The bay is protected by huge rocks but plants are sprouting up between them. Nature's habit of reclaiming. I stand on the short pier and look back towards Tankerton, buffeted by the wind. But I'm rewarded with a grey-satin, luminescent sea and the sun back-lighting a band of black cloud creating a curious peephole of blue sky and a figure-of-eight-shaped dazzle in the grey clouds either side of the blackness.

My return is slower, heading into the wind. I watch children play in the park that was formerly an oyster breeding pool. A flock of starlings pecks in the grass and another flock flits and flies from beach huts to ground and back to beach hut roofs. I almost squash a caterpillar on the concrete path. A huge hairy thing about five centimetres long, its presence is a mystery as there's no nearby vegetation.

I'm nearly back at my hut when I'm overtaken by a man on a skateboard. There's nothing so unusual about that; plenty head to and from their park's ramps and slopes. But this man has a pole which he ingeniously uses like a punt pole. All power to his elbow.

Another day I walk to the brook and I discover that a large semicircle has been excavated. The earth's piled high and caterpillar-tyre tracks mark the dried-up ground. It looks like a medieval defensive works. What's its purpose? Several months later, in winter, I return. The earthworks are full of water. They're not linked to the brook but the water-table in the area has risen so that a lake's emerged. It's a simple way of controlling the marshiness of the marsh – the water gathering in one place ensures the other ground remains relatively un-boggy.

During my residency, I only explore a small part of Long Rock mainly on the look-out for birds. It's one of the areas of the north Kent coast where migratory birds shelter for the winter. The following April, at the spring tide, a friend and I don wellington boots and go investigating. Brent geese peck at the seaweed. I suspect it won't be long before they fly north. The tide's receded, revealing a broken waste pipe marked with a red buoy. We head towards it and are glad of wellies so we can splash through the surface water, our footprints puddling and disappearing. The clay oozes and sometimes we stick in the black gunk underneath.

The landscape appears dull brown and grey, in many ways unwelcoming, but this habitat hides a multitude of fascinations: mudstones, cracked apart, looking like broken bones, and shellfish galore – knuckled slipper limpets; solitary camouflaged oysters; razor shells poking up through the mud or pocked circles revealing their hidden whereabouts; whelks, including one who at that precise moment is secreting her eggs; and the broken pipe is home for a mussel colony.

We walk past a couple of fishermen. Their haul, stashed in a wheelbarrow and bucket, contains two huge rays, a dogfish and several enormous cockles. We see bright orange sponges, mermaid's purses and many kinds of seaweed. It seems an alien place but we are not alone; more than once we're asked what we've discovered. So enthused by all I've seen I open my mouth to reply, but hesitate, unsure of which to choose. However one such conversation reveals they assume we are fossil-hunters. A man relates the whole list of his finds from this stretch of coast.

I'm amazed at the variety, more or less on my doorstep. I thought I'd discovered so much during the residency but here are many new things. This place, that at first glance appears unappealing, hides a treasure trove. The cloud-covered sky accentuates an eerie atmosphere. It reminds me of the time when I wrote in my journal that the sky is *overcast* and then began to puzzle over the word's definitions.

Mackerel Scales and Mares' Tails

make lofty ships carry low sails.[1]

Overcast – my dictionary at the Little Blue Hut gives nine definitions: "to overthrow; to cast as a covering; to cast a covering over; to shade; to sew stitches over (a raw edge); to cover with stitches; to recover, get over; to compute too high, overestimate; to grow dull and cloudy, (adj) clouded over, (n) a cloudy covering". That's quite some list of which only the last is to do with clouds.[2]

When I get home, I look in another dictionary[3] – again there are nine definitions. But they're not the same nine: "covered over or obscured, especially by clouds; (meteorol, of the sky) more than 95% cloud-covered; gloomy or melancholy; sewn over by overcasting; (vb) to make or become overclouded or gloomy; to sew (an edge, as of a hem) with long stitches passing successively over the edge; (n) a covering, as of clouds or mist; (meteorol) the state of the sky when more than 95% of is cloud-covered; (mining) a crossing of two passages without an intersection". I've gained a more precise definition concerning cloud cover and one concerning mine passages, but there's nothing about staging a coup, being unrealistic in estimates or using a throw to hide a worn sofa.

Words – the playthings of writers. With so many definitions a poet can manipulate double, triple (nine-fold) meanings. But in general conversation, I'd guess the most common use of overcast concerns the weather. Today, before starting to write, I glance out of the window and the sky is overcast (though I doubt whether that's meteorologically accurate). I don't feel gloomy, haven't been stitching, nor has the radio news reported that Robert Mugabe is ousted from power.

Half an hour later, I glance up again and the sky is blue with only a few scattered clouds. Why the change? What is a cloud anyway?

> A cloud is a visible air-borne suspension of particles, usually water droplets or ice crystals. Their size varies from less than a micrometre (0.001 millimetres) to up to about 100 micrometres. A wide range of particles is the rule. Drops larger than about 100 micrometres are not held in suspension but fall out as mist or rain. All cloud particles drift slowly downward; water drops about 1 micrometre across descend at only a fraction of a millimetre per second and so are lofted indefinitely at the whims of air currents. The 100 micrometre variety falls at about 30 centimetres per second.[4]

From this scientific definition, we learn that clouds are made from water or ice and hang in the air. But that's hardly sufficient to describe the different displays which cause me to reach for a camera or scribble in my journal. Nor does it explain how clouds gather and disperse, or why they generally appear white or grey. Richard Hamblyn's *The Invention of Clouds,*[5] tells how clouds came to be named, classified and understood. The protagonist of the story is Luke Howard, a young Quaker man, who from boyhood was fascinated by cloud shapes and shifts.

At the turn of the nineteenth century a fervour for scientific knowledge gripped educated and self-educated men. New ideas were propounded almost daily. Each had potential to increase man's understanding and enable him to modify and control his world. People paid to hear science lectures and see experiments, and subscribed to one or more of the many scientific journals.

On a December evening in 1802, in the basement of a building in Plough Court, London, Luke Howard presented *On the Modification of Clouds.* At the time, the most popular theory for cloud formation was the vesicular or 'bubble' theory which maintained that water particles formed into hollow spherules through the action of the sun. These were filled with an 'aura' of highly rarefied, lighter air which rose like a hot-air balloon and formed into clouds.

Luke Howard had a different idea. Through years of watching the skies he'd noticed that though clouds may adopt innumerable shapes, they could be classified into a few forms. He suggested that both shape and form were affected by conditions in the atmosphere and more specifically by temperature, humidity and pressure. As air cools, its capacity to hold water vapour decreases until, at its dewpoint, the vapour condenses as droplets around airborne particles such as sea salt, pollen, dust or smoke. These tiny water droplets bundle together in their billions to form clouds. If the air temperature is sufficiently low, then clouds are composed of ice crystals.

Every cloud is in a constant state of turmoil. Even low-lying clouds that appear static are actually changing. Some water evaporates from them but more is added by absorption from the earth's surface. Wind in the upper air can alter cloud shapes and cause them to 'fly' across the sky. And they rain. All water droplets gradually sink, larger ones faster than smaller. Some droplets also coalesce with others. Once a cloud has too many large droplets, it can no longer hold them and so rain falls.

But Howard not only explained how clouds formed and modified; he named them. He categorised three basic types:[6]

> Cirrus: (Latin for a curl of hair), which he described as "parallel, flexuous, or diverging fibres, extensible in any or all directions".
> Cumulus: (meaning heap), which he described as "convex or conical heaps, increasing upward from a horizontal base".
> Stratus: (meaning something spread), described as "a widely extended, continuous, horizontal sheet, increasing from below".

He suggested four modifications:

> Cirro-cumulus: "small, well-defined roundish masses, in close horizontal arrangement".
> Cirro-stratus: "horizontal or slightly inclined masses, attenuated towards a part or the whole of their

> circumference, bent downward, or undulated, separate, or in groups consisting of small clouds having these characters".
>
> Cumulostratus: "the cirrostratus blended with the cumulus, and either appearing intermixed with the heaps of the latter, or super-adding a widespread structure to its base".
>
> Cumulo-cirro-stratus or Nimbus: which he called the rain cloud, "a cloud or system of clouds from which rain is falling". He described it as "a horizontal sheet, above which the cirrus spreads, while the cumulus enters it laterally and from beneath".

Seven forms to classify all the many shapes. Howard stressed that clouds are not immutable – they can change from one form into another or disappear completely. He illustrated his lecture with pencil sketches, washed with watercolour, so his audience would be certain of his clouds. His ideas quickly became popular, aided by the championing of a forceful science publisher, Alexander Tilloch. Howard's cloud definitions began to be used by newly-established meteorological stations and other weather enthusiasts. He wasn't without naysayers – some thought his classification was not thorough enough; others thought that Latin names were inappropriate for modern England.

But Howard's names have stuck – not only in England but worldwide. They have undergone modification: Howard's cumulo-stratus was switched to stratocumulus to describe a layer of cloud not flat enough to be stratus and not bumpy enough to be cumulus. By 1896, which was nominated as the International Year of Clouds, there were 10 classifications according to their altitude:[7]

A: Upper Clouds (altitude 9000m)

1. Cirrus
2. Cirro-stratus

B: Intermediate Clouds (altitude between 3000 and 7000m)

3. Cirro-cumulus
4. Alto-cumulus
5. Alto-stratus

C: Lower Clouds (2000m)

6. Strato-cumulus
7. Nimbus

D: Clouds of diurnal or Ascending Currents

8. Cumulus: apex 1800m, base 1400m
9. Cumulo-nimbus: apex 3000-8000m, base 1400m

E: High Fogs (under 1000m)

10. Stratus

"Being on cloud nine" originated with this classification – cumulo-nimbus is the highest climbing cloud. Subsequent classifications ranked it at number 10 but the saying somehow stuck. Other sub-categories have been introduced and there's no better way of getting to grips with them than in Richard Hamblyn's *The Cloud Book*.[8] I can't praise his two books highly enough for clarity and information. They have transformed my understanding of clouds.

The Cloud Book is filled with pages of colour photographs. I can match my photos to his (sky not scenery, obviously) and discover which clouds I've seen. Mares' tails are wispy cirrus clouds. Mackerel scales are cirrocumulus or altocumulus clouds which are small, white and fluffy and usually formed from ice crystals. With patches of blue sky peeping between the clouds they are supposed to look like the scales on a mackerel fish. I'm not convinced – to me they look like cotton wool balls, but I guess that reflects my urban upbringing. Apparently in Germany and France, they are known as sheep cloud.

There's nothing quite like watching clouds floating by in a blue sky. Probably most of us at some time or another have played shape-spotting. One day I was waiting for a friend at Samphire Hoe. As I looked out over the sea the beginnings of a poem crept to the edges of my imagination:

Sway

I'm gazing on a tide-high sea
of undulating soft hued blue,

a horizon garnished with cumuli
whose shapes could have you recognising

whales or bears or nesting birds
or sub-Saharan Africa.

Higher the sky is cirrus-striped,
cradling a glamorous silver sun

which casts a glitter so sparkly bright
that my un-shaded eyes

can only rest on it fleetingly.
Moments like this are sustenance

in which I slip from afflicting guilt
that other lives are pained and stressed.

Samphire Hoe is a rather special place on the south Kent coast. It's a completely artificial landscape, created from the debris left by the construction of the Channel Tunnel and made into a nature reserve with an abundance of birds and plants including samphire.[9] We both bought small potted samphire plants that day. Mine seems to thrive better in a Ramsgate coastal garden than my friend's at Maidstone.

The sky's blue is due to the scattering and absorption of white light in the atmosphere. Blue is scattered most frequently. Clouds don't absorb light. Each individual cloud particle is spherical and so scatters light a little. But the combined effect of the billions of particles leads to no overall scattering and so clouds appear white.

But they aren't all white. In England we are all too familiar with a grey day. Dark clouds aren't composed of dirty water. Shadows cause the grey. In a sky filled with many clouds, sunlight cannot penetrate to the lower ones – they are literally in the shadow of the higher clouds. Also in a thick cloud, self-shadowing may occur – the upper layers prevent light penetrating the lower cloud. A thin cloud can also be dark as it will not only transmit sunlight but also some of the background sky-light. This, being blue, causes the cloud to appear darker.

Clouds are often transformed at sunrise and sunset into a glorious display of colours: pink, yellow, orange, red and mauve. The clouds may be illuminated by coloured light; they may be translucent and allow coloured background light through; or when seen at a distance through air, the shorter wavelengths of light are absorbed and so reds and yellows become more dominant.[10]

We don't need to know the science to enjoy watching a sunset or to revel in the cloud formations of a gathering storm. Clouds can help predict forthcoming weather. Mares' tails and mackerel scales are evidence of strong high-level winds which may foretell a depression on its way and stormy weather – hence the need for lofty ships to lower their sails. With online and 24-hour television access to forecasts we no longer need to interpret 'the signs' but sitting in a beach hut, with no electricity, I become attentive to weather fronts arriving – massing clouds, rain falling and rainbows on the horizon. I also become fascinated by how clouds affect the colour of the sea.

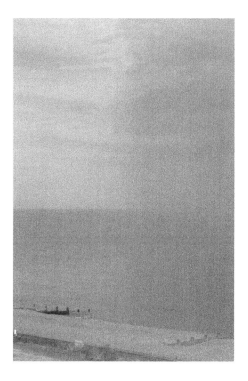

Watercolours

To paint the sea really well, you need to look at it every hour of every day in the same place so that you can understand its ways in that particular spot.

Claude Monet [1]

So what colour is the sea? Some observations from my journal read:

> The sky is definitely blue; the sea is still – a murmuring of blue and brown.

The sea is more luminous now – I think that's the right word – it has a shiny effect and is more blue than brown.

It has changed again – the blue has lightened.

More blue than brown. More grey in the blue than brown in the blue today.

On the horizon is a band of grey – roofing/asphalt grey. The sea's lighter nearer the shore – air-force blue maybe. There's still a tinge of brown in it.

And we're hitting white-out… the sea is losing colour, not pastelling but like it's been invaded by white; though you couldn't call it white. And once it starts raining the sea appears lighter not darker… It's brightening again – colours are getting deeper – more blue in the sea – an incredibly pretty colour just now.

Cloud-free sky and the colour of the sea has become more various – patches of deeper blue with turquoise.

It's a blue/brown mix – more blue than brown… Sea is grey changing to blue slate – I like that colour… Sea is green/grey with a touch of brown and deep blue on the horizon…

The sea seemed to celebrate the season's turn with its brightest hues of blue and green.

The sea's becoming bluer – hints of white and green.

The sea has a band of white and blue amongst much deeper blue… becoming more turquoise… blue/jade now…

It's a gorgeous day and the sea is like baby-blue emulsion paint.

There's black in the green in the blue… Still black in the green in the blue… Some white horses further out where brown is mixed with green.

The sea is blue/grey with hints of brown and near the horizon hints of green… And in under a minute the sea is streaked with green.

Blue in the brown – no, brown in the blue, with odd streaks of green. Clouds cause ever-changing patterns… Grey, grey sky and sea but never just one colour.

Sea is brown and blue today with a dark blue band at the horizon… An incredibly vivid blue sky to the east and the sea's turning green… I can't keep up with all the changes…

The sea is almost brown, vivid blue has gone. And it all happens whether or not anybody is looking on.

Large patch of reddish brown in the greeny-brown sea; near the horizon grey/black, and cloud shadows are navy blue…

Underneath a wave is blue, the top of the wave is brown with white as it crashes on to the shore.

> The clouds are 'drawing' colour from the sea which is a light greeny-grey with touches of yellow, apart from a dark brownish band blurring the horizon. I'm intrigued by the sea colour near the shore – striations of blue and yellowy-blue. I would definitely paint the sea with yellow in today.
>
> An interesting shape on the sea – like a huge grey lustrous flying bird on a silver sea…Blue sky spreading from the west – the sea is becoming greener with a brown-yellow patch on the western horizon… I can draw a line down through the sky and sea – so blue to the west, so green to the east; and slate blue and grey on west and east horizons.
>
> The sea's so green under dark grey cloud… sea is a light green ripple… sea is a grey sheen – blue in centre, green to east and grey to the west.

These are a selection of my scribblings. Like Monet, I feel the need to observe again and again. It's so difficult to know the sea. Words keep reappearing – brown, blue, grey, yellow, black, pastel, luminous, turquoise, jade, in different combinations. The frequent changes leave me wondering how an artist chooses a palette for a seascape. Twenty minutes later, or even ten or five, the scene may be very different.

The Impressionists liked to paint 'en plein air' to capture both the nature and the atmosphere of a place.

> The painter [Monet] lurked in front of his subject, waiting for sun and shadow; with a few strokes of the brush he caught a beam of light or passing clouds… Another time, he dragged down with his hands a

> shower of rain sweeping across the sea and smacked it on to the canvas.
>
> **Guy de Maupassant, 1886**[2]

Authors, too, may use colour to reflect mood as well as reality:

> …that vast bowl of water bulging like a blister, lead-blue and malignantly agleam…
> …we swam at night, the water flowing over our arms like undulations of black satin…
>
> from **The Sea** by John Banville[3]

I surf the Internet for techniques on painting the sea. One site suggests using Idanthrene blue, Prussian blue, ultramarine, cerulean blue, cobalt turquoise, cobalt teal, phtalo blue red shade, green gold and phtalo green blue shade – though not all at the same time.[4] Another has a palette foundation of cadmium yellow light, cadmium red, manganese blue, burnt sienna and titanium white, with mixes of all of these.[5] Paints may be used as solid colour, more thinly as glaze or blended together.

> Sea with waves does not have a universal colour, but he who sees it from dry land sees it dark in colour and it will be so much darker to the extent that it is closer to the horizon, [though] he will see there a certain brightness or lustre which moves slowly in the manner of white sheep in flocks… from the land [you] see the waves reflect the darkness of the land, and from the high sea [you] see in the waves the blue air reflected…
>
> **Leonardo da Vinci, 1452-1519**[6]

Where you place the shore in a picture is important as this affects the waves' direction. It's also necessary to consider the position of the light as corresponding shadows will alter colours, as will the relative amounts of sunshine and cloud. There are many articles and DVD or YouTube clips available to aid a budding seascape painter. But they're beyond my capability. Instead, I take photos in an attempt to capture the sea's hues and moods.

When water flows from a tap, whether to fill a kettle, mop bucket or glass, it's transparent, and near the shore the sea is clear; we see the bottom of the seabed through the shallow water. So why does the sea appear coloured? Generally, a large body of water appears blue; the thicker the bluer. Water absorbs light of longer wavelengths (red and orange) more easily than shorter wavelengths (blue). The thicker the water the more absorption occurs and the bluer it appears. Therefore, we see the sea as blue. Well, sometimes…

Other factors also influence. Light (and therefore the colour we see) comes from three different places in the water:

> reflected from the surface;
>
> refracted through the top, scattered within the body of the water, then refracted back through the surface;
>
> refracted through the top, transmitted by the water to the bottom where it is reflected back up through the water and then is refracted a second time at the air-water interface.

Each of these has a greater or lesser influence dependent upon the conditions. In shallow water, light from the bottom is most important; in deep clear water, surface reflections are brightest and in muddy water the light is scattered by the sediment.[7]

The colours of the sea I predominantly see from my beach hut are the effects of reflected sky-light – blue sky, blue sea; overcast sky, greyer sea, with clouds creating patterns of colours, though often it is difficult to match up any particular cloud with its shadow on the sea. When white clouds hang low, with an approaching storm, they create an effect of colour being leached from the sea. Brown, often part of the sea-colour mix, is probably due to light scattered by suspended particles or reflected from the bottom clay as the waters are relatively shallow.

On windier days, white horses gallop and waves leave foam as they break on the shore. These are white for the same reason that clouds are white – the light is scattered by spheres. Clouds are water spheres held in air; foam and white horses are air spheres held in water, but the effect is the same. The combined scattering of all the bubbles means we see them as white. Particles held within the water can give foam a yellow tinge.[8]

At sunrise and sunset, the sea can reflect the colour changes of the dawn and dusk sun and sky. I witness many scenes worthy of an Impressionist painting and I'm inspired to capture the colours in photos and words. The water turns orange, red, pink and tangerine, pastel or fiery.

I fall in love with glitter. A low sun above water that is wind-ruffled produces a path of sparkling light. The sea acts as a million little mirrors which create sun glints – instantaneous flashes of sunlight reflected from waves at just the right slope and position to send the light in my direction. The colour of glitter varies with the sun's colour and can also occur when a bright moon is over the sea.[9] So many times I need to stop, stare and marvel. I wonder if I'm becoming like Robin Robertson's fishermen in his "The Fishermen's Farewell".[10]

> Their long stares mark them apart; eyes gone
> to sea colours: grey, foam-flecked
>
> and black in the undertow, blue
> as the blue banners of the mackerel, whipping west.

Sometimes the sea transforms to an oily or satin sheen. Rougher water and a high sun create numerous reflections which appear and disappear in an instant. This is so different to the thick emulsion paint effect I saw when the sky was a rich blue and the sea very calm. And that is so different to the brown days when it appears sediment rules the waves. And that is so different…

I could continue with many versions. There's so much to watch and absorb. I've learnt some explanations for the sea's moods and colours which increase my desire and fascination to experience them. I've seen cat's paws, moon circles, the caustic network and boat masts wiggling in the water. Whenever I spend time by the sea, something grabs my attention. I came across R.S. Thomas' poem *Tidal* in which he compares prayer with the tide's continual approach and retreat. [11] I attempt a response to his poem based on the sea's changing colours:

Watercolour

…Let despair be known
as my ebb-tide; but let prayer
have its springs, too…
R.S. Thomas

The colours of the sea shift
within moments of a day.
My desires and needs behave
the same. The water turns
from brown to green, blue to grey
to combinations of all these
or sunset's golds, pinks, tangerine.
It changes whether anybody sees.
I must imitate it only
in refraction and reflection
of my environment's intricacies,
not in its inconsistency.
Sometimes prayer is dull; sometimes
I churn and toss petitions
flimsy as froth; sometimes
there's glitter, a myriad mirror
images of the Sun. Only
in returning day after day, year in
year out, I may comprehend
a bigger picture.

Sea Change

Full fathom five thy father lies;
Of his bones are coral made;
Those are pearls that were his eyes:
Nothing of him that doth fade,
But doth suffer a sea-change
Into something rich and strange…

Ariel's song** from **The Tempest Act I, Scene 2[1]

The sea can symbolize both constancy and change. It's always present, ebbing and flowing on the shore. It causes erosion and deposition. It carries generation after generation of living organisms within its depths. It's littered with natural debris, with flotsam and jetsam, and with other man-made waste – bottled messages, oil slicks, undegradable plastic... Its appearance, sound and temperament change with its environment. The sea can be blessing or curse: bring bounty and adventure or flood and shipwreck. And through centuries we have exploited, explored and researched it, and by so doing have aided and damaged this great natural wealth.

In *The Tempest* Ariel tries to comfort Ferdinand for the death of his father at sea. He sings of how the father's body will change into something permanent, *rich and strange*. This seems to be the origin of the phrase sea-change, seachange or sea change meaning "a seemingly magical change brought about by the action of the sea"[2] or more abstractedly "a poetic or informal term meaning a gradual transformation in which the form is retained but the substance replaced"[3]. We use the phrase to define something that's effected a change in our behaviour, paradigms or circumstances.

The residency at the Little Blue Hut created a sea change in me. It was a catalyst for an ongoing transformation from ignoramus to appreciator to continuing learner of sea and shore. W.H. Auden infamously said "poetry makes nothing happen", but without this residency, during which I could contemplate colour and write poetry, my sea change may never have begun, my poetry remained unwritten, and this book, *The Sea Changes,* wouldn't have come to birth. Auden wrote the phrase within a poem about the death of the poet W.B. Yeats:[4]

You were silly like us; your gift survived it all:
The parish of rich women, physical decay,
Yourself. Mad Ireland hurt you into poetry.
Now Ireland has her madness and her weather still,
For poetry makes nothing happen: it survives
In the valley of its making where executives
Would never want to tamper, flows on south
From ranches of isolation and the busy griefs,
Raw towns that we believe and die in; it survives,
A way of happening, a mouth.

Far from belittling poetry, in its context the phrase suggests that poetry has an importance of its own and will survive, beyond the interference of executives, to express the emotion of our lives – give happenings a mouth. Many times during my residency I doubted the usefulness of my being there. I didn't know if it would result in any vibrant poetry or whether I was wasting six weeks of my time in vain pursuit. Our capitalist and efficiency mind-sets have become hardwired to measure outcomes and results in terms of productivity, not by life-affirmation, connectedness or understanding. But "What is this life if, full of care,/ We have no time to stand and stare?"

This was possibly a once-in-a-lifetime opportunity. The Little Blue Hut is no longer available for residencies and I now have different claims on my time. Amongst the doubts and internal clamour for proof of achievement, I learnt to listen to the 'still, small voice' and trust that as I waited, watched and fed, something would happen. I am not sure whether I achieved my original intentions; I still feel inept at describing colour – but in the weeks and months following the residency, *Little Blue Hut,* a collection of poetry emerged. *The Sea Changes* also germinated from a desire to share the delights of my discoveries and hopefully to inspire others on a similar journey – or rather a similar standing still.

One of my mother's legacies (apart from Fields' stand and stare poetry) is a belief that we can tackle anything. She was a product of her childhood through the war – make do and mend, be inventive and creative in finding solutions to problems – and she lived this philosophy throughout her life. She didn't baulk from decorating and gardening; jam-making and preserving; from teaching us to read long before we reached school-age; from making our wedding dresses and decorating the wedding-cakes; from encouraging us to enter competitions – I remember the day when she received a letter saying she had won £5000. And I was the proud owner of a portable black-and-white TV courtesy of UHU glue which survived through teenage, university and into the first years of married life.

For her, difficulties were part of life's rich tapestry and there to be surmounted or walked around; difficulties which included raising four children whilst being afflicted by paralysing bouts of multiple sclerosis. She was an incredibly intelligent woman but I mainly saw her philosophy worked out in practical ways. Whether by nature or nurture she planted those seeds of 'tackle-ability' in me. As I grew up I followed a science route (probably also because of my mother's influence) but with her attitude embedded in me, much later in life, I laid down science and had the courage to begin to explore writing and poetry. But it doesn't need to be either/or, it can be both/and…

The more you learn, the more you realise there is to learn. We can only ever be experts in a very small area, if we ever reach that status, but I love gaining even a little knowledge about anything; it brings joy, increases my appreciation. Is it part of human nature to want to know and categorise or just part of my character?

> we always think that we are looking on looking in
>
> sand scutter snake snout-mouse
> if we speak them they will be –
> and made ours by the arrangement…
>
> yet we are made lonely by our categories
> for nothing else owns them
>
> from **'by categories do we maister [master] the world'**
> by Jeffrey Wainwright [5]

I love this poem by Wainwright, the idea "that it is in us to see". I understand his notion that in naming we set ourselves apart but, for me, it is in seeing, naming and categorising that I begin to feel re-connected with the world and less willing to trample it with devastating real or carbon footprints. Everywhere holds something for us to discover, whether countryside, seashore, mountain, village or city. It is a case of 'he who has eyes to see…' Tankerton Slopes is, at the same time, both unique and not at all. The *Fisher's estuarine moth* and The Street are almost unique to the area – the moth exists in only one other place; shingle spits may be plentiful but never quite the same. Other things can be found commonly – crows, gulls, shingle and the sea. But these can be enjoyed within a particular environment. My awakening at Tankerton has enabled me to take delight in other locations – my hometown of Ramsgate; the windmills of Kent (inspired by comparison with the white ladies), the woods around Canterbury, the wilds of Dungeness...

The current trend is to visit inspirational locations, fuelled by such books as *Unforgettable things to do before you die* or *1000 Places to See Before you Die.*[6] We must traipse across the world, gain the experience, cross it off the list. Our tales from Machu Picchu, the Pyramids, the Grand Canyon, a Las Vegas Casino or Ibiza nightclub make for good dinner party or pub conversation. It seems certain places signify achievement. I'm no party pooper – I would love to visit some of those sights. But if we are always hankering after the BIG experience, we can fail to see what's under our noses or take delight in the little (and not so little) things on our doorsteps.

I'm not aiming to preach but my awakening has turned me into a missionary for others to know similar experiences. My residency at the Little Blue Hut was a joy-filled, life-affirming, re-connecting time. I would wish the same for anyone. I am grateful to *Creative Canterbury* of Canterbury City Council for awarding the residency.

Invocation

Absorbed by change's constancy:
moon rise and size, tide time and height,
shingle's shift and revealed spit
patterning the waters' drift,
resident birds, transient people,
sun's arc, haze, mist and rainbows;
cirrus and cumulus cover, clear
and with the sun, churn of waves,
a kaleidoscopic sea array.
Charmed by nature's alchemy
let constant change be berthed in me

Notes

Town Girl by the Sea

1. *Leisure,* written by W.H. Davies (1871-1940), first appeared in *Songs of Joy and Others* in 1911. Originally born in Wales, Davies spent much of his early adult life tramping across America. The poet, Edward Thomas, helped Davies in his writing career and by providing him with a home near his own in Sevenoaks, Kent.

Beach Huts

1. A *Short History of Beach Huts* by Kathryn Ferry can be found at http://www.beach-huts.com/history-of-beach-huts.php
2. Information about Canterbury City Council's Beach Hut sites can be found at

https://www.canterbury.gov.uk/leisure-countryside/foreshore-services/beach-huts/

3. Frank W. Harvey's *Ducks* was written whilst in a prisoner of war camp during WWI. It became part of his collection *Ducks* that was published in 1919.
4. Details for renting *Beacon House* can be found at http://www.thebeaconhouse.co.uk/

Settling In

1. In this traditional song, the animals actually go into the ark in increasingly higher numbers *for to get out of the rain.*
2. Gage, John: *Colour and Meaning: Art, Science and Symbolism*: Thames & Hudson, Ltd., 1999: pp. 23-24
3. Ibid. pp. 90-91
4. Ibid. pp. 24-26

Moon Shine Moon Time

1. Several nursery rhymes feature the moon. For example: *Hey diddle diddle, the cat and the fiddle, the cow jumped over the moon; Girls and boys come out to play the moon does shine as bright as day…*
2. Quoted in: *Collins Spacewatching: The Ultimate Guide to the Stars and Beyond:* O'Bryne, J (consulting ed.): HarperCollins, 1998: p. 95
3. Moon and sun rise and set times can be found at www.timeanddate.com
4. *Spacewatching:* p. 90

5. Levy, David: *Collins Skywatching: The Ultimate Guide to the Universe:* HarperCollins, 1995: p. 92
6. Muirden, James: *Astronomy with a Small Telescope,* George Philip Ltd., 1985: pp. 48-49
7. Jones, Emma: *The Striped World:* Faber and Faber Ltd., 2009: p. 1
8. Found in: Tripp, Rhoda Thomas: *The International Thesaurus of Quotations:* Penguin Books Ltd., 1976: p. 412
9. http://www.celticmythmoon.com/moon.html for a selection of full moon names.
10. http://en.wikipedia.org/wiki/Full_moon provides information about the full moon including blue moons.
11. http://www.dailymail.co.uk/news/article-2193749/Neil-Armstrong-speech-Thats-small-step-man-famous-mankind-words-misquoted.html reveals how Armstrong always claimed that he has said 'a man' but that no-one heard that transmitted.
12. For all things Wallace and Gromit go to http://www.wallaceandgromit.com. This lovable, inventive pair were created by Nick Park.
13. *Spacewatching:* p. 92
14. Ibid. p. 92
15. Ibid. p. 94
16. Ibid. p. 93
17. See such websites as http://www.guardian.co.uk/science/brain-flapping/2012/dec/13/moon-landings-faked-science-confessions and http://en.wikipedia.org/wiki/Moon_landing_conspiracy_theories for conspiracy theory possibilities.

18. For examples of current research see this article: http://www.guardian.co.uk/commentisfree/2012/nov/23/moon-lunacy-study
19. Lynch, David K. and Livingston, William: *Color and Light in Nature:* Cambridge University Press, 1995: pp. 124-127

Of Crows, Gulls and Cormorants

1. Hughes, Ted: *Crow: From the Life and Songs of the Crow:* Faber & Faber Ltd., 1972: p. 3
2. Various mythologies about the crow can be discovered at http://paganwiccan.about.com/od/othermagicspells/p/The-Magic-Of-Crows-And-Ravens.htm
3. Gooders, John: *Pocket Guide: Birds of Britain and Ireland:* Larousse plc, 1995: p. 228
4. The earliest known citation of the phrase, which explicitly defines its meaning, comes in *The London Review Of English And Foreign Literature*, by W. Kenrick, 1767: 'The Spaniaad [sic], if on foot, always travels as the crow flies, which the openness and dryness of the country permits; neither rivers nor the steepest mountains stop his course, he swims over the one and scales the other.' http://www.phrases.org.uk/meanings/as-the-crow-flies.html
5. Bach, Richard: *Jonathan Livingston Seagull: a story*: HarperElement, 2003. The original version first came out in 1970.
6. Morgan, Lee: *Coastal Birds:* AA Media Limited, 2011: pp. 134-135

7. With many thanks to Kim Norton, Education Officer at Dover Museum, for help with remembering the names.
8. Discover the lovely Harbour Books at 21 Harbour Street, Whitstable, Kent, CT5 1AQ
9. Morgan: pp. 56-57
10. Robertson, Robin: *The Wrecking Light:* Picador, 2010. The poem *At Roane Head*, dedicated to John Burnside, tells the story of a woman whose sons were more fish than men…

Aliens

1. http://corporate.vattenfall.co.uk/projects/operational-wind-farms/kentish-flats/. In February 2013 permission was granted to extend Kentish Flats by a further 17 turbines.
2. http://en.wikipedia.org/wiki/Wind_power_in_the_United_Kingdom. At the beginning of 2013 the UK was ranked as the eighth largest producer of wind power.
3. Project Redsand can be found at http://www.project-redsand.com/history.htm revealing plans for the future but also packed full of the history of these fascinating structures.
4. For a detailed history of the piers that have been at Herne Bay go to https://en.wikipedia.org/wiki/Herne_Bay_Pier
5. Sheppey has its own website. The detail about passports can be found here: http://www.sheppeywebsite.co.uk/index.php?id=77
6. Lynch, David K. & Livingston, William: *Color and Light in Nature:* Cambridge University Press, 1995: pp. 24-26. This

book became a much-read companion during my residency and I still dip into it to remind me of some of the fascinating phenomena in nature.

Defences

1. Oliver, Mary: *Wild Geese:* Bloodaxe Books Ltd., 2004: p. 133. My favourite (and most challenging) lines in this lovely poetry book come from the poem *The Summer Day. 'Tell me, what is it that you plan to do/ with your one wild and precious life?'*
2. Jennings, Simon: *Collins Artist's Little Book of Colour:* Collins, 2007; Barber, John: *Water Colour: a visual reference to mixing water colours:* Search Press Ltd., 2006.
3. Collins Dictionary, 2007: p. 722
4. Details of the Coastal Defence Scheme can be found out http://www.se-coastalgroup.org.uk/tankerton-coastal-scheme/ and https://www.canterbury.gov.uk/leisure-countryside/coastal-management/coastal-defence-works/tankerton-coastal-defence-scheme-phase-i-and-ii/
5. Goodall, Robert H, *The Whitstable Copperas Industry,* Archaeologia Cantiana Vol. 70, 1956, found online at http://www.kentarchaeology.org.uk/Research/Pub/ArchCant/Vol.070%20-%201956/070-05.pdf

Tide and Time Wait for No Man

1. Banville, John: *The Sea:* Picador, 2005: pp. 3-4
2. Pictures and stories of the Whitstable flood can be found at the informative website:

http://www.simplywhitstable.com/flood1953/flood53ppage/flood53ppage.html

3. The same site also provides pictures of a frozen Whitstable at http://www.simplywhitstable.com/frozensea/fr-frame.htm
4. We thought the winter of 2012/3 was bad but really it was nothing in comparison with 1962/3 http://www.lancashiretelegraph.co.uk/bygones/11673424.Frozen_in_time_______some_scenes_from_our_very_chilly_past/
5. Thomas, R.S.: *Collected Later Poems 1988 - 2000:* Bloodaxe Books Ltd., 2004: p. 63
6. Current tide timetables can be found here: https://www.thebeachguide.co.uk/south-east-england/kent/tankerton-beach-weather.htm
7. Pretor-Piney, Gavin: *The Wavewatcher's Companion*: Bloomsbury Publishing plc, 2010: pp. 223-227
8. Many books and websites give explanations of the moon and sun's gravitational pull and of other factors that affect the tides. One that explains mathematically but quite simply is http://www.math.ubc.ca/~cass/courses/m309-01a/lai/formation.html
9. For diagrams and explanations of different tides go to http://www.physicalgeography.net/fundamentals/8r.html
10. Pretor-Piney: pp. 250-251
11. Kemp, Peter (ed.): *The Oxford Companion to Ships and the Sea,* Oxford University Press, 1976: p. 808
12. http://en.wikipedia.org/wiki/Tide. The explanation occurs in the section on timing.

13. A helpful notice by the east harbour wall at Whitstable provides information about the incoming and outgoing tides.

The Street

1. Martin Knight on his eclectic website provides an interesting article about the North Kent coast... http://www.martindknight.co.uk/HerneBay.html
2. Under an excellent photograph of the tide receding on the spit, Martin Knight provides this helpful information about the colours of the stones.
3. From the websites explaining about longshore drift it becomes obvious that it is a topic taught in school geography. For a sample try http://www.bbc.co.uk/education/clips/zk6myrd, http://en.wikipedia.org/wiki/Spit_(landform) and, of course, Martin Knight at http://www.martindknight.co.uk/HerneBay.html
4. http://en.wikipedia.org/wiki/Spit_(landform). I also checked this out in my Collins dictionary which agrees. It's so satisfying to discover a new word or a new meaning for a word.

Cockles and Mussels Alive and Dead

1. The battle between the slipper limpets and oysters is told at http://www.glaucus.org.uk/oyster2.htm

2. Another trip to Harbour Books resulted in buying Ken Preston-Mafham's *Collins Nature Guide: Seashore of Britain and Europe*. Slipper limpets can be found on page 184. Other interesting slipper limpet information can be discovered from: Will Rayment, 2008. *Crepidula fornicata*. Slipper limpet. Marine Life Information Network: Biology and Sensitivity Key Information Sub-programme [on-line]. Plymouth: Marine Biological Association of the United Kingdom. [cited 29/04/2013]. Available from: http://www.marlin.ac.uk/speciesfullreview.php?speciesID=3086
3. Wrongly informed of the tide times by their gangmaster and unable to understand others who tried to warn them, the cockle pickers were caught out by the rapid return of the flowing tide.
4. It is fun looking up the aetiology of phrases on the Internet and seeing the variation of ideas. One site for 'cockles of the heart' is http://www.innovateus.net/innopedia/what-does-warm-cockles-your-heart-mean
5. Cockle information was found in the Collins Book, p. 207 and here: Dr Harvey Tyler-Walters, 2007. *Cerastoderma edule*. Common cockle. Marine Life Information Network: Biology and Sensitivity Key Information Sub-programme [on-line]. Plymouth: Marine Biological Association of the United Kingdom. [cited 29/04/2013]. Available from: http://www.marlin.ac.uk/speciesfullreview.php?speciesID=2924.
6. Collins: p. 202
7. Collins: p. 179

8. From *The Parasite* by *Sir Arthur Conan Doyle* found at http://www.classic-literature.co.uk/scottish-authors/arthur-conan-doyle/the-parasite/ebook-page-02.asp
9. Collins: p. 190 and also at: http://www.glaucus.org.uk/Buckie.htm, and http://www.asnailsodyssey.com/LEARNABOUT/WHELK/whelFeed.php
10. Collins: p. 231 and also at: http://www.glaucus.org.uk/Mermaid.htm

The World's Mine Oyster

1. Act II Scene II opens with Falstaff refusing to lend Pistol a penny. Pistol replies: *Why, then the world's mine oyster,/ Which I with sword will open./ I will retort the sum in equipage.*
2. http://h2g2.com/approved_entry/A283105 for a more comprehensive review of oysters in British history.
3. Preston-Mafham, Ken: *Collins Nature Guides: Seashore of Britain and Europe:* HarperCollins Publishers Ltd., 2008: p. 206
4. http://www.glaucus.org.uk/oyster2.htm for much information on oysters and their lives and times…
5. http://www.simplywhitstable.com/ for numerous stories told and retold by Whitstable residents past and present.
6. The story of the *Favourite* and other oyster boats can be found at http://www.simplywhitstable.com/oysterdredging/oysterboats/oysterboats.html

7. http://www.whitstableoystercompany.com/ for the official website of the Whitstable Oyster Company.
8. http://www.whitstableoysterfestival.com/ is the official website of the annual Whitstable Oyster Festival.

An Aggregate Harbour

1. You can find the story of Brett Aggregates at http://www.whitstablescene.co.uk/harbour1.htm
2. www.whitstableharbour.org for facts, figures and stories about the harbour.
3. The stage at Dead Man's Corner was erected in 2011. Local people helped make some of its pebbles. See http://www.kentonline.co.uk/kentish_gazette/man_serious_after_assault/2011/april/26/harbour.aspx and http://www.geograph.org.uk/photo/2674754
4. http://www.whitstableharbourvillage.co.uk/ gives details of this enterprise.
5. By the boat there is a container with pamphlets about the Greta. You can also find out more at www.greta1892.co.uk
6. You can hear Derek West talk about his experiences at www.westwhelks.co.uk.
7. Grateful thanks to Jane and Pete Findlay for solving my duck mystery.
8. Information about the lifeboat can be found at www.whitstablelifeboat.org.uk.
9. Armac Marine were registered in Rochester and then in Bromley but went into dissolution in 2012. However, the Falcon has been sighted and photographed: www.shipspotting.com.

10. It's www.whitstableharbour.org that provided this information.

Birds of a Feather…

1. Morgan, Lee: *Coastal Birds:* AA Media Limited, 2011: pp. 106-7
2. Ibid. pp. 138-193
3. Robertson, Robin: *The Swithering:* Picador, 2006: pp. 35-6
4. *Coastal Birds:* pp. 72-3
5. Oliver, Mary: *Wild Geese:* Bloodaxe Books Ltd, 2004.: p. 21.
6. *Coastal Birds:* pp. 10-11

Michaelmas Day

1. http://wiki.answers.com/Q/What_is_St_Michael_the_Archangel_the_patron_saint_of for the comprehensive list.
2. http://www.historic-uk.com/CultureUK/Michaelmas.htm provides information about the history of Michaelmas Day
3. http://projectbritain.com/calendar/September/Michaelmas.html is another good resource not only about Michaelmas Day but also other traditions.
4. The feast of St Simon and St Jude is traditionally celebrated on 28th October.
5. Ecclesiastes 11:1, New International Version.

Seaside Special

1. http://en.wikipedia.org/wiki/Seaside_Special is where I discovered the little information that I found.
2. You-tube clips can be found at: http://www.youtube.com/watch?v=8B5v5CL9hx4, http://www.youtube.com/watch?v=JoxhoEYmikw and others besides…
3. Lynch, David K and Livingston, William: *Color and Light in Nature,* Cambridge University Press, 1995
4. Ibid. pp. 31-32 for information on the colour and brightness of the low sun, and the aureole.
5. Ibid. p. 47 for the 'flattened' sun.
6. Ibid. pp. 34-38 for twilight.
7. Collins Artist's Little Book of Colours: pp. 81-85
8. Gage, John: *Colour and Meaning: Art, Science and Symbolism*: Thames & Hudson, Ltd., 1999: p. 28
9. https://www.dulux.co.uk/en/colour-palettes for those yellow inspirations.
10. http://en.wikipedia.org/wiki/List_of_colors:_A-F for colours from A-F. Of course, there are other lists for the rest of the alphabet.
11. *Color and Light in Nature:* p. 42

Season's Turn

1. *A time to be born and a time to die,/ a time to plant and a time to uproot,/ a time to kill and a time to heal…* And so Ecclesiastes chapter 3 continues, reminding us of the breadth and depth of life.

2. http://en.wikipedia.org/wiki/Marathon. During the 1960s women first took part in marathon races.
3. http://en.wikipedia.org/wiki/Turn!_Turn!_Turn! Seeger's only additions to the biblical words are the phrases *Turn, turn, turn* and *I swear it's not too late.*
4. http://en.wikipedia.org/wiki/Equinox
5. As above, plus http://earthsky.org/?p=26181 and http://news.nationalgeographic.com/2016/09/autumn-equinox-explained-start-fall-spring-sun-earth-science/
6. http://horsebridge-centre.org.uk/ is the Horsebridge Arts and Community Centre website where you can find out about all the various activities that it hosts. To discover more about the redevelopment of the Horsebridge area go to http://webarchive.nationalarchives.gov.uk/20110118095356/http://www.cabe.org.uk/case-studies/horsebridge-development/evaluation
7. http://www.seewhitstable.com/Whitstable_alleys.html for information of Whitstable's many alley ways. Better still, go and explore them for yourself.

Migration, Murmuration and Mystery

1. Gooders, John: *Larousse Pocket Guide, Birds of Britain and Ireland:* Larousse plc, 1995. This book, alongside Lee Morgan's: *AA Spotter Guide, Coastal Birds:* AA Media Limited, 2011 and Detlef Singer's: *Collins Nature Guides, Garden Birds of Britain & Europe*: HarperCollins Publisher Ltd., 2011, provided much of the bird information in this chapter.

http://sussexhistoryforum.co.uk/index.php?topic=446.0 which also lists archival material about the castle held at Canterbury Cathedral Archives.

The Circus is in Town

1. *A-Z Street Atlas: Margate, Ramsgate, Canterbury, Whitstable:* Geographers' A-Z Map Company Limited, 2000: pp. 8-11
2. *Collins Dictionary:* HarperCollins Publishers, 2007: p. 321
3. Pearson, Anya and Coldwell, Will (eds.): *#5 inc. magazine, Poetry and Illustration, The Postcard Issue (May 2012).*
4. http://www.oystertown.net/oystertown-news/peggotty-house/ gives the story of Peggoty House.
5. http://www.countyestateagents.co.uk/tankerton-estates are the current managers of 'The Tankerton Estate'.
6. This website http://www.kentpast.co.uk/swalecliffe.html gives a brief description of Swalecliffe's past.

Slope Dwellers

1. *Collins Dictionary:* HarperCollins Publishers, 2007: p. 822
2. http://www.seaview-cafe.co.uk/ The café specialises in traditional English food and provides a great cooked breakfast for those so inclined.
3. http://www.tbsc.co.uk/ – the website for Tankerton Bay Sailing Club.
4. http://www.nci.org.uk/whitstable for Whitstable Coastwatch details.

5. Tankerton Conservation Appraisal, Canterbury City Council, March 2, 2010: p. 5; found online at: https://www.canterbury.gov.uk/media/215230/tankerton-consarea-appraisal.pdf
6. Webster, Jean: *Daddy-Long-Legs*: Hodder & Stoughton. My copy does not give date of publishing but it was first published in 1912 and is still in print.
7. Hughes, Ted: *Collected Poems:* Faber & Faber, 2012 (ebook)
8. http://www.rspb.org.uk/birds-and-wildlife/bird-and-wildlife-guides/a-z-of-a-wildlife-garden/atoz/c/cranefly.aspx gives some information about the crane fly life cycle.
9. www.telegraph.co.uk/news/earth/wildlife/3307701/Crane-fly-emerging-later-due-to-climate-change.html for a fascinating article on the changes in crane fly habits.
10. http://webarchive.nationalarchives.gov.uk/20140605090108/http://www.naturalengland.org.uk/Images/tankerton-sad_tcm6-32905.pdf gives details of the proposition to create the Slopes into a SSSI.
11. http://www.arkive.org/fishers-estuarine-moth/gortyna-borelii-lunata/ provides photographs and information about the moth.

Hoar Strange and Brimstonewort

1. http://botanical.com/botanical/mgmh/f/fenhog05.html and http://www.essexbiodiversity.org.uk/species-and-habitats/trees-and-plants/sea-hogs-fennel provide information about hog's fennel and the Fisher's Estuarine Moth.

2. *Collins Dictionary:* HarperCollins Publishers, 2007: p. 1744
3. http://botanical.com/botanical/mgmh/f/fenhog05.html again.
4. McClintock, David and Fitter, R.S.R: *Collins Pocket Guide to Wild Flowers:* Collins, 1972, p.101-2. This provided Gerard's quote. I found out more about him and his amazing work at http://en.wikipedia.org/wiki/John_Gerard.
5. Preston-Mafham, Ken: *Collins Nature Guides, Seashore of Britain & Europe:* HarperCollins Publishers Ltd., 2008: p. 49
6. http://seedystories.blogspot.co.uk/2012/07/plant-profile-yellow-horned.html Here is a true lover of yellow horned poppies.
7. http://psychoactiveherbs.com/catalog/index.php?cPath=170_193
8. http://www.plantlife.org.uk/wild_plants/plant_species/yellow_horned-poppy
9. Robert Bridges' poem can be found online at http://www.bartleby.com/360/5/204.html. It is part of: Bliss, Carmen et al. (eds.): *The World's Best Poetry. Volume V. Nature,* 1904.
10. Fitter, Richard & Fitter, Alastair: *Collins Pocket Guide, Wild Flowers of Britain and Northern Europe:* HarperCollins Publishers, 1993; p. 260. It is interesting to see the variations between this edition and the earlier 1972 (originally printed in 1955) edition. Put together they provide a better insight than either does separately but then I suppose that reflects the limitations of a pocket guide.
11. Sterry, Paul & Cleave, Andrew: *Collins Complete Guide to British Coastal Wildlife:* HarperCollins Publishers, 2012, p. 92. This is a delightful modern addition to Collins Guides.

12. *Seashore of Britain and Europe:* p. 56. *British Coastal Wildlife:* p. 70
13. http://www.gallowaywildfoods.com/sea-kale-identification-edibility-and-distribution/ and http://www.eattheweeds.com/sea-kale/ for the history and culinary delights of sea kale.
14. *British Coastal Wildlife:* p. 60. *Wild Flowers* (1972)*:* p. 44
15. All the above mentioned guides have aided in my growing (if still paltry) knowledge of plant species.
16. *Seashore of Britain and Europe*: p. 88.

Holdfasts for Bladders, Gut and Belt

1. http://oceanservice.noaa.gov/facts/seaweed.html is a page on the website of the United States National Oceanic and Atmospheric Administration which tells something of the interesting history of seaweed; as does http://en.wikipedia.org/wiki/Edible_seaweed
2. Sterry, Paul & Cleave, Andrew: *Collins Complete Guide to British Coastal Wildlife:* HarperCollins Publishers, 2012; pp. 26-7 gives a good introduction to seaweeds.
3. http://www.seaweed.ie/ Whatever you look up about seaweed on the Internet you are most often directed or linked to *The Seaweed Site.*
4. For this and all my other identifications I am indebted to the *Collins Complete Guide to British Coastal Life:* pp. 28-41 and to the *Collins Nature Guides: Seashore of Britain and Europe:* pp. 10-44.

5. http://www.thanet.gov.uk/news/focus_on_news/seaweed_in_thanet.aspx for explanations and control of Thanet's seaweed.
6. http://en.wikipedia.org/wiki/Elegiac_couplet for explanation of elegiac couplets.

There's Nowt So Queer as Folk

1. This is a traditional saying – one of those my mother would quote frequently.
2. http://en.wikipedia.org/wiki/Fl%C3%A2neur will provide with some basic information about being a flâneur if you care to embark on such a 'career'.
3. *Lowry and the Painting of Modern Life:* Exhibition leaflet, 2013. In the exhibition, there was a couple of seaside paintings (unusual for Lowry), one of which was entitled, *Lytham 1963*. We went to my grandparents at Lytham St. Anne's each summer. I was born in 1963 so possibly I was there in my pram when Lowry painted this picture.
4. Michael Blumenthal: *What I Believe* found in: Astley, Neil (ed.): *Being Human:* Bloodaxe Books Ltd., 2011: p. 40
5. Eliot, T.S.: *The Love Song of J. Alfred Prufrock* found in: Astley, Neil (ed.): *Being Human:* Bloodaxe Books Ltd., 2011: pp. 34-37

Open Day

1. *Collins Dictionary:* HarperCollins Publishers, 2007: p. 151
2. Ibid. p. 304

3. *Chromatography* can be found at http://www.nancycharley.blogspot.co.uk/
4. http://www.the-piedpiper.co.uk/th11f.htm is a fascinating website for all things arachnoid.
5. Professor Fritz Volraith, an evolutionary biologist, explores the possibilities for using spider silk in medicine. www.theguardian.com/science/2013/jan/12/fritz-vollrath-spiders-tim-adams
6. The 'pied piper' again provides the information as does Collins dictionary the definitions.
7. Woolf, Virginia, *The Waves,* Vintage, 2004 (Kindle edition): p. 153
8. http://en.wikipedia.org/wiki/The_Waves provides a basic introduction to the book.

From Long Rock to Hampton Bay

1. The tale of Hampton-on-Sea can be found at http://en.wikipedia.org/wiki/Hampton-on-Sea and http://www.abandonedcommunities.co.uk/hampton.html
2. Percy Bysshe Shelley's *Ode to the West Wind* I found in: *The Great Writers: Romantic Poets, An Anthology:* Marshall Cavendish Partworks Ltd., 1987: pp. 192-195.
3. http://www.walkingclub.org.uk/clothes-free/beach/Long_Rock_Beach_Swalecliffe_Kent.shtml for details.

Mackerel Scales and Mares' Tails

1. This traditional proverb has many variations – mackerel skies, mare's tails, tall ships, lower sails. The version I chose seemed, to me, to be the most poetic (and grammatically correct).
2. *Chambers English Dictionary,* 1988: p. 1023
3. *Collins Dictionary,* 2007: p. 1160
4. Lynch, David K. & Livingston, William: *Color and Light in Nature:* Cambridge University Press, 1995: p. 133
5. Hamblyn, Richard: *The Invention of Clouds:* Picador, 2001. This book is a real delight. In well-written prose Hamblyn tells the story not only of Luke Howard's 'invention' of clouds but the surrounding bigger picture. I thoroughly recommend it.
6. These descriptions of Howard's clouds were taken from http://www.rmets.org/weather-and-climate/observing/luke-howard-and-cloud-names
7. Hamblyn, Richard: *The Cloud Book: How to Understand the Skies:* David and Charles Limited, 2008: p.12
8. http://www.samphirehoe.com/uk/home/
9. With Hamblyn's two books anybody can gain a 'grounding' in clouds.
10. *Color and Light in Nature:* pp. 134-139

Watercolours

1. I discovered this quote as the epigraph of Tobias Hill's delightful poetry book, *Nocturne in Chrome & Sunset Yellow:* Salt Publishing, 2006.

2. Zeidler, Birgit: *Claude Monet: Life and Work:* Könemann Verlagsgesellschaft mBH, 2000: p. 57.
3. Banville, John: *The Sea:* Picador, 2005: pp. 3, 135.
4. http://painting.about.com/od/landscapes/ss/paint_sea.htm. On this site Marion Boddy-Evans provides colours and also considerations of position and light.
5. http://www.artinstructionblog.com/seascape-painting-lesson-by-brian-oliver
6. Kemp, Martin: *Leonardo on Painting: Anthology of Writings by Leonardo Da Vinci with a Selection of Documents Relating to His Career as an Artist:* Yale University Press, 2001: p.170
7. Lynch, David K. & Livingston, William: *Color and Light in Nature:* Cambridge University Press, 1995: pp. 65-67
8. Ibid. p. 92
9. Ibid. p. 77
10. *The Fisherman's Farewell,* from Robertson, Robin: *Hill of Doors*: Picador, 2013: p. 21
11. Thomas, R.S.: *Collected Later Poems: 1988-2000*: Bloodaxe Books Ltd., 2004: p. 167

Sea Change

1. Shakespeare, William: *The Complete Works:* Murray Sales and Services Co., 1978: p. 14.
2. *Collins Dictionary,* 2007: p. 1454.
3. https://en.wikipedia.org/wiki/Sea_change_(idiom)
4. I found Auden's wonderful three part poem, *In Memory of W.B. Yeats,* at http://www.poets.org/viewmedia.php/prmMID/15544

5. Wainwright, Jeffrey: *Clarity or Death!*: Carcanet Press Limited, 2008: p. 27
6. There is an abundance of such books. The two mentioned are: Watkins, Steve and Jones, Clare: *Unforgettable Things to do before you die:* BBC Books, 2005, and Schultz, Patricia: *1000 Places to See Before you Die:* Workman Publishing, 2003.

#0051 - 220617 - C0 - 210/148/12 - PB - DID1875154

2. Oliver, Mary: *Owls and Other Fantasies: Poems and Essays:* Beacon Press, 2006 (Kindle edition)
3. http://www.lastwordonnothing.com/2013/01/15/murmuration-the-poetry-of-the-morning-walk/
4. http://www.rspb.org.uk/wildlife/birdguide/name/s/starling/roosting.aspx
5. http://www.telegraph.co.uk/earth/wildlife/4736472/The-mathematics-of-murmurating-starlings.html
6. http://www.rspb.org.uk/wildlife/birdguide/name/r/rockpipit/index.aspx
7. Burnside, John: *Gift Songs:* Jonathan Cape, 2007: p. 37
8. www.stagcottage.co.uk tells the story from the owner's perspective.

Initiation Rites

1. These quotes are mainly from traditional nursery rhymes: Ring-a ring o' roses, The Grand Old Duke of York, and Jack and Jill climbed up the hill. 'Spinning and spinning and spinning around' is from another of those songs for which I can remember the first two lines and have them incessantly run through my head but can't actually place its origins. Any ideas?
2. Information about the pudding pots can be found at http://www.bbc.co.uk/ahistoryoftheworld/objects/a-ndhydOTDyvfZZ-GzW8pw
3. This quote comes from http://www.whitstablecastle.co.uk/the-castle
4. All the information is taken from the Whitstable castle website above and from